Epistles, Elegies, Epitaphs & Pastorals by John Dryden

John Dryden was born on August 9th, 1631 in the village rectory of Aldwincle near Thrapston in Northamptonshire. As a boy Dryden lived in the nearby village of Titchmarsh, Northamptonshire. In 1644 he was sent to Westminster School as a King's Scholar.

Dryden obtained his BA in 1654, graduating top of the list for Trinity College, Cambridge that year.

Returning to London during The Protectorate, Dryden now obtained work with Cromwell's Secretary of State, John Thurloe.

At Cromwell's funeral on 23 November 1658 Dryden was in the company of the Puritan poets John Milton and Andrew Marvell. The setting was to be a sea change in English history. From Republic to Monarchy and from one set of lauded poets to what would soon become the Age of Dryden.

The start began later that year when Dryden published the first of his great poems, Heroic Stanzas (1658), a eulogy on Cromwell's death.

With the Restoration of the Monarchy in 1660 Dryden celebrated in verse with Astraea Redux, an authentic royalist panegyric.

With the re-opening of the theatres after the Puritan ban, Dryden began to also write plays. His first play, The Wild Gallant, appeared in 1663 but was not successful. From 1668 on he was contracted to produce three plays a year for the King's Company, in which he became a shareholder. During the 1660s and '70s, theatrical writing was his main source of income.

In 1667, he published Annus Mirabilis, a lengthy historical poem which described the English defeat of the Dutch naval fleet and the Great Fire of London in 1666. It established him as the pre-eminent poet of his generation, and was crucial in his attaining the posts of Poet Laureate (1668) and then historiographer royal (1670).

This was truly the Age of Dryden, he was the foremost English Literary figure in Poetry, Plays, translations and other forms.

In 1694 he began work on what would be his most ambitious and defining work as translator, The Works of Virgil (1697), which was published by subscription. It was a national event.

John Dryden died on May 12th, 1700, and was initially buried in St. Anne's cemetery in Soho, before being exhumed and reburied in Westminster Abbey ten days later.

Index of Contents
EPISTLES.
Epistle I. To John Hoddeson
Epistle II. To Sir Robert Howard
Epistle III. To Dr Charleton

Epistle IV. To the Lady Castlemain
Epistle V. To Mr Lee
Epistle VI. To the Earl of Roscommon
Epistle VII. To the Duchess of York
Epistle VIII. To Mr J. Northleigh
Epistle IX. To Sir George Etherege
Epistle X. To Mr Southerne
Epistle XI. To Henry Higden, Esq
Epistle XII. To Mr Congreve
Epistle XIII. To Mr Granville
Epistle XIV. To Mr Motteux
Epistle XV. To Mr John Driden
Epistle XVI. To Sir Godfrey Kneller
ELEGIES AND EPITAPHS.
Upon the Death of Lord Hastings
To the Memory of Mr Oldham
To the Pious Memory of Mrs Anne Killigrew
Upon the Death of the Viscount of Dundee
Eleonora, A Panegyrical Poem, to the Memory of the Countess of Abingdon
Dedication to the Earl of Abingdon
On the Death of Amyntas
On the Death of a very young Gentleman
Upon young Mr Rogers of Gloucestershire
On the Death of Mr Purcell
Epitaph on the Lady Whitmore,
Mrs Margaret Paston
Epitaph on the Monument of the Marquis of Winchester
Sir Palmer Fairbones' tomb in Westminster Abbey
The Monument of a fair Maiden Lady
Inscription under Milton's Picture
PASTORALS
Pastoral I. or, Tityrus and Meliboeus
Pastoral II. or, Alexis
Pastoral III. or, Palaemon.
Pastoral IV. or, Pollio
Pastoral V. or, Daphnis
Pastoral VIII. or, Pharmaceutria
Pastoral IX. or, Lcyidas and Moeris
Pastoral X. or, Gallus
JOHN DRYDEN – A SHORT BIOGRAPHY
JOHN DRYDEN – A CONCISE BIBLIOGRAPHY

EPISTLES.

EPISTLE THE FIRST,

TO HIS FRIEND JOHN HODDESDON, ON HIS DIVINE EPIGRAMS.

Thou hast inspired me with thy soul, and I,
Who ne'er before could ken of poetry,
Am grown so good proficient, I can lend
A line in commendation of my friend.
Yet 'tis but of the second hand; if ought
There be in this, 'tis from thy fancy brought.
Good thief, who dar'st, Prometheus-like, aspire,
And fill thy poems with celestial fire;
Enlivened by these sparks divine, their rays
Add a bright lustre to thy crown of bays.
Young eaglet, who thy nest thus soon forsook,
So lofty and divine a course hast took,
As all admire, before the down begin
To peep, as yet, upon thy smoother chin;
And, making heaven thy aim, hast had the grace
To look the sun of righteousness i'the face.
What may we hope, if thou goest on thus fast?
Scriptures at first, enthusiams at last!
Thou hast commenced, betimes, a saint; go on,
Mingling diviner streams with Helicon,
That they who view what epigrams here be,
May learn to make like, in just praise of thee.—
Reader, I've done, nor longer will withhold
Thy greedy eyes; looking on this pure gold,
Thou'lt know adulterate copper; which, like this,
Will only serve to be a foil to his.

EPISTLE THE SECOND.

TO MY HONOURED FRIEND SIR ROBERT HOWARD, ON HIS EXCELLENT POEMS.

As there is music uninformed by art
In those wild notes, which, with a merry heart,
The birds in unfrequented shades express,
Who, better taught at home, yet please us less;
So in your verse a native sweetness dwells,
Which shames composure, and its art excells.
Singing no more can your soft numbers grace,
Than paint adds charms unto a beauteous face.
Yet as when mighty rivers gently creep,
Their even calmness does suppose them deep,
Such is your muse: no metaphor swelled high
With dangerous boldness lifts her to the sky:
Those mounting fancies, when they fall again,

Show sand and dirt at bottom do remain.
So firm a strength, and yet withal so sweet,
Did never but in Sampson's riddle meet.
'Tis strange each line so great a weight should bear,
And yet no sign of toil, no sweat appear.
Either your art hides art, as stoics feign
Then least to feel, when most they suffer pain;
And we, dull souls, admire, but cannot see
What hidden springs within the engine be:
Or 'tis some happiness, that still pursues
Each act and motion of your graceful muse.
Or is it fortune's work, that in your head
The curious net that is for fancies spread,
Lets through its meshes every meaner thought,
While rich ideas there are only caught?
Sure that's not all; this is a piece too fair
To be the child of chance, and not of care.
No atoms, casually together hurled,
Could e'er produce so beautiful a world;
Nor dare I such a doctrine here admit,
As would destroy the providence of wit.
'Tis your strong genius, then, which does not feel
Those weights, would make a weaker spirit reel.
To carry weight, and run so lightly too,
Is what alone your Pegasus can do.
Great Hercules himself could ne'er do more,
Than not to feel those heavens and gods he bore.
Your easier odes, which for delight were penned,
Yet our instruction make their second end;
We're both enriched and pleased, like them that woo
At once a beauty, and a fortune too.
Of moral knowledge poesy was queen,
And still she might, had wanton wits not been;
Who, like ill guardians, lived themselves at large,
And, not content with that, debauched their charge.
Like some brave captain, your successful pen
Restores the exiled to her crown again;
And gives us hope, that having seen the days
When nothing flourished but fanatic bays,
All will at length in this opinion rest,—
"A sober prince's government is best."
This is not all; your art the way has found
To make improvement of the richest ground;
That soil which those immortal laurels bore,
That once the sacred Maro's temples wore.
Eliza's griefs are so expressed by you,
They are too eloquent to have been true.
Had she so spoke, Æneas had obeyed

What Dido, rather than what Jove, had said.
If funeral rites can give a ghost repose,
Your muse so justly has discharged those,
Eliza's shade may now its wandering cease,
And claim a title to the fields of peace.
But if Æneas be obliged, no less
Your kindness great Achilles doth confess;
Who, dressed by Statius in too bold a look,
Did ill become those virgin robes he took.
To understand how much we owe to you,
We must your numbers, with your author's, view:
Then we shall see his work was lamely rough,
Each figure stiff, as if designed in buff;
His colours laid so thick on every place,
As only showed the paint, but hid the face.
But, as in perspective, we beauties see,
Which in the glass, not in the picture, be;
So here our sight obligingly mistakes
That wealth, which his your bounty only makes.
Thus vulgar dishes are, by cooks, disguised,
More for their dressing than their substance prized.
Your curious notes so search into that age,
When all was fable but the sacred page,
That, since in that dark night we needs must stray,
We are at least misled in pleasant way.
But, what we most admire, your verse no less
The prophet than the poet doth confess.
Ere our weak eyes discerned the doubtful streak
Of light, you saw great Charles his morning break:
So skilful seamen ken the land from far,
Which shows like mists to the dull passenger.
To Charles your muse first pays her duteous love,
As still the ancients did begin from Jove;
With Monk you end, whose name preserved shall be,
As Rome recorded Rufus' memory;
Who thought it greater honour to obey
His country's interest, than the world to sway.
But to write worthy things of worthy men,
Is the peculiar talent of your pen;
Yet let me take your mantle up, and I
Will venture, in your right, to prophecy:—
"This work, by merit first of fame secure,
Is likewise happy in its geniture;
For since 'tis born when Charles ascends the throne,
It shares at once his fortune and its own."

EPISTLE THE THIRD.

TO MY HONOURED FRIEND DR CHARLETON, ON HIS LEARNED AND USEFUL WORKS, BUT MORE PARTICULARLY HIS TREATISE OF STONEHENGE, BY HIM RESTORED TO THE TRUE FOUNDER.

The longest tyranny that ever swayed,
Was that wherein our ancestors betrayed
Their free-born reason to the Stagyrite,
And made his torch their universal light.
So truth, while only one supplied the state,
Grew scarce, and dear, and yet sophisticate.
Still it was bought, like emp'ric wares, or charms,
Hard words sealed up with Aristotle's arms.
Columbus was the first that shook his throne,
And found a temperate in a torrid zone:
The feverish air, fanned by a cooling breeze;
The fruitful vales, set round with shady trees;
And guiltless men, who danced away their time,
Fresh as their groves, and happy as their clime.
Had we still paid that homage to a name,
Which only God and nature justly claim,
The western seas had been our utmost bound,
Where poets still might dream the sun was drowned;
And all the stars, that shine in southern skies,
Had been admired by none but savage eyes.
Among the assertors of free reason's claim,
Our nation's not the least in worth or fame.
The world to Bacon does not only owe
Its present knowledge, but its future too.
Gilbert shall live, till loadstones cease to draw,
Or British fleets the boundless ocean awe.
And noble Boyle, not less in nature seen,
Than his great brother, read in states and men.
The circling streams, once thought but pools, of blood,
(Whether life's fuel, or the body's food,)
From dark oblivion Harvey's name shall save;
While Ent keeps all the honour that he gave.
Nor are you, learned friend, the least renowned;
Whose fame, not circumscribed with English ground,
Flies like the nimble journies of the light,
And is, like that, unspent too in its flight.
Whatever truths have been, by art or chance,
Redeemed from error, or from ignorance,
Thin in their authors, like rich veins of ore,
Your works unite, and still discover more.
Such is the healing virtue of your pen,
To perfect cures on books, as well as men.
Nor is this work the least; you well may give

To men new vigour, who make stones to live.
Through you, the Danes, their short dominion lost,
A longer conquest than the Saxons boast.
Stonehenge, once thought a temple, you have found
A throne, where kings, our earthly gods, were crowned;
Where by their wondering subjects they were seen,
Joyed with their stature, and their princely mien.
Our sovereign here above the rest might stand,
And here be chose again to rule the land.
These ruins sheltered once his sacred head,
When he from Wor'ster's fatal battle fled;
Watched by the genius of this royal place,
And mighty visions of the Danish race.
His refuge then was for a temple shown;
But, he restored, 'tis now become a throne.

EPISTLE THE FOURTH.

TO THE LADY CASTLEMAIN, UPON HER ENCOURAGING HIS FIRST PLAY, THE WILD GALLANT, ACTED IN 1662-3.

As seamen, shipwrecked on some happy shore,
Discover wealth in lands unknown before;
And, what their art had laboured long in vain,
By their misfortunes happily obtain:
So my much-envied muse, by storms long tost,
Is thrown upon your hospitable coast,
And finds more favour by her ill success,
Than she could hope for by her happiness.
Once Cato's virtue did the gods oppose;
While they the victor, he the vanquished chose;
But you have done what Cato could not do,
To choose the vanquished, and restore him too.
Let others still triumph, and gain their cause
By their deserts, or by the world's applause;
Let merit crowns, and justice laurels give,
But let me happy by your pity live.
True poets empty fame and praise despise,
Fame is the trumpet, but your smile the prize.
You sit above, and see vain men below
Contend for what you only can bestow;
But those great actions others do by chance,
Are, like your beauty, your inheritance:
So great a soul, such sweetness joined in one,
Could only spring from noble Grandison.
You, like the stars, not by reflection bright,

Are born to your own heaven, and your own light;
Like them are good, but from a nobler cause,
From your own knowledge, not from nature's laws.
Your power you never use, but for defence,
To guard your own, or others' innocence:
Your foes are such, as they, not you, have made,
And virtue may repel, though not invade.
Such courage did the ancient heroes show,
Who, when they might prevent, would wait the blow;
With such assurance as they meant to say,
We will o'ercome, but scorn the safest way.
What further fear of danger can there be?
Beauty, which captives all things, sets me free.
Posterity will judge by my success,
I had the Grecian poet's happiness,
Who, waving plots, found out a better way;
Some God descended, and preserved the play.
When first the triumphs of your sex were sung
By those old poets, beauty was but young,
And few admired the native red and white,
Till poets dressed them up to charm the sight,
So beauty took on trust, and did engage
For sums of praises till she came to age.
But this long-growing debt to poetry,
You justly, madam, have discharged to me,
When your applause and favour did infuse
New life to my condemned and dying muse.

EPISTLE THE FIFTH.

TO MR LEE, ON HIS TRAGEDY OF THE RIVAL QUEENS, OR ALEXANDER THE GREAT. 1677.

The blast of common censure could I fear,
Before your play my name should not appear;
For 'twill be thought, and with some colour too,
I pay the bribe I first received from you;
That mutual vouchers for our fame we stand,
And play the game into each others hand;
And as cheap pen'orths to ourselves afford,
As Bessus and the brothers of the sword.
Such libels private men may well endure,
When states and kings themselves are not secure;
For ill men, conscious of their inward guilt,
Think the best actions on by-ends are built.
And yet my silence had not 'scaped their spite;
Then, envy had not suffered me to write;

For, since I could not ignorance pretend,
Such merit I must envy or commend.
So many candidates there stand for wit,
A place at court is scarce so hard to get:
In vain they crowd each other at the door;
For e'en reversions are all begged before:
Desert, how known soe'er, is long delayed,
And then, too, fools and knaves are better paid.
Yet, as some actions bear so great a name,
That courts themselves are just, for fear of shame;
So has the mighty merit of your play
Extorted praise, and forced itself a way.
'Tis here as 'tis at sea; who farthest goes,
Or dares the most, makes all the rest his foes.
Yet when some virtue much outgrows the rest,
It shoots too fast, and high, to be supprest;
As his heroic worth struck envy dumb,
Who took the Dutchman, and who cut the boom.
Such praise is yours, while you the passions move,
That 'tis no longer feigned, 'tis real love,
Where nature triumphs over wretched art;
We only warm the head, but you the heart.
Always you warm; and if the rising year,
As in hot regions, brings the sun too near,
'Tis but to make your fragrant spices blow,
Which in our cooler climates will not grow.
They only think you animate your theme
With too much fire, who are themselves all phlegm.
Prizes would be for lags of slowest pace,
Were cripples made the judges of the race.
Despise those drones, who praise, while they accuse,
The too much vigour of your youthful muse.
That humble style, which they your virtue make,
Is in your power; you need but stoop and take.
Your beauteous images must be allowed
By all, but some vile poets of the crowd.
But how should any sign-post dauber know
The worth of Titian, or of Angelo?
Hard features every bungler can command;
To draw true beauty, shews a master's hand.

EPISTLE THE SIXTH.

TO THE EARL OF ROSCOMMON, ON HIS EXCELLENT ESSAY ON TRANSLATED VERSE.

Whether the fruitful Nile, or Tyrian shore,

The seeds of arts and infant science bore,
'Tis sure the noble plant, translated first,
Advanced its head in Grecian gardens nurst.
The Grecians added verse; their tuneful tongue
Made nature first, and nature's God their song.
Nor stopt translation here; for conquering Rome,
With Grecian spoils, brought Grecian numbers home;
Enriched by those Athenian muses more,
Than all the vanquished world could yield before.
Till barbarous nations, and more barbarous times,
Debased the majesty of verse to rhymes;
Those rude at first; a kind of hobbling prose,
That limped along, and tinkled in the close.
But Italy, reviving from the trance
Of Vandal, Goth, and Monkish ignorance,
With pauses, cadence, and well-vowel'd words,
And all the graces a good ear affords,
Made rhyme an art, and Dante's polished page
Restored a silver, not a golden age.
Then Petrarch followed, and in him we see,
What rhyme improved in all its height can be;
At best a pleasing sound, and fair barbarity.
The French pursued their steps; and Britain, last,
In manly sweetness all the rest surpassed.
The wit of Greece, the gravity of Rome,
Appear exalted in the British loom:
The Muses' empire is restored again,
In Charles his reign, and by Roscommon's pen.
Yet modestly he does his work survey,
And calls a finished poem an essay;
For all the needful rules are scattered here;
Truth smoothly told, and pleasantly severe;
So well is art disguised, for nature to appear.
Nor need those rules to give translation light;
His own example is a flame so bright,
That he, who but arrives to copy well,
Unguided will advance, unknowing will excel.
Scarce his own Horace could such rules ordain,
Or his own Virgil sing a nobler strain.
How much in him may rising Ireland boast,
How much in gaining him has Britain lost!
Their island in revenge has ours reclaimed;
The more instructed we, the more we still are shamed.
'Tis well for us his generous blood did flow,
Derived from British channels long ago,
That here his conquering ancestors were nurst,
And Ireland but translated England first:
By this reprizal we regain our right,

Else must the two contending nations fight;
A nobler quarrel for his native earth,
Than what divided Greece for Homer's birth.
To what perfection will our tongue arrive,
How will invention and translation thrive,
When authors nobly born will bear their part,
And not disdain the inglorious praise of art!
Great generals thus, descending from command,
With their own toil provoke the soldier's hand.
How will sweet Ovid's ghost be pleased to hear
His fame augmented by an English peer;
How he embellishes his Helen's loves,
Outdoes his softness, and his sense improves?
When these translate, and teach translators too,
Nor firstling kid, nor any vulgar vow,
Should at Apollo's grateful altar stand:
Roscommon writes; to that auspicious hand,
Muse, feed the bull that spurns the yellow sand.
Roscommon, whom both court and camps commend,
True to his prince, and faithful to his friend;
Roscommon, first in fields of honour known,
First in the peaceful triumphs of the gown;
Who both Minervas justly makes his own.
Now let the few beloved by Jove, and they
Whom infused Titan formed of better clay,
On equal terms with ancient wit engage,
Nor mighty Homer fear, nor sacred Virgil's page:
Our English palace opens wide in state,
And without stooping they may pass the gate.

EPISTLE THE SEVENTH.

TO THE DUCHESS OF YORK, ON HER RETURN FROM SCOTLAND, IN THE YEAR 1682.

When factious rage to cruel exile drove
The queen of beauty, and the court of love,
The Muses drooped, with their forsaken arts,
And the sad Cupids broke their useless darts;
Our fruitful plains to wilds and desarts turned,
Like Eden's face, when banished man it mourned.
Love was no more, when loyalty was gone,
The great supporter of his awful throne.
Love could no longer after beauty stay,
But wandered northward to the verge of day,
As if the sun and he had lost their way.
But now the illustrious nymph, returned again,

Brings every grace triumphant in her train.
The wondering Nereids, though they raised no storm,
Foreslowed her passage, to behold her form:
Some cried, A Venus; some, A Thetis past;
But this was not so fair, nor that so chaste.
Far from her sight flew Faction, Strife, and Pride;
And Envy did but look on her, and died.
Whate'er we suffered from our sullen fate,
Her sight is purchased at an easy rate.
Three gloomy years against this day were set;
But this one mighty sum has cleared the debt:
Like Joseph's dream, but with a better doom,
The famine past, the plenty still to come.
For her, the weeping heavens become serene;
For her, the ground is clad in cheerful green;
For her, the nightingales are taught to sing,
And Nature has for her delayed the spring.
The Muse resumes her long-forgotten lays,
And Love restored his ancient realm surveys,
Recals our beauties, and revives our plays,
His waste dominions peoples once again,
And from her presence dates his second reign.
But awful charms on her fair forehead sit,
Dispensing what she never will admit;
Pleasing, yet cold, like Cynthia's silver beam,
The people's wonder, and the poet's theme.
Distempered zeal, sedition, cankered hate,
No more shall vex the church, and tear the state;
No more shall faction civil discords move,
Or only discords of too tender love:
Discord, like that of music's various parts;
Discord, that makes the harmony of hearts;
Discord, that only this dispute shall bring,
Who best shall love the duke, and serve the king.

EPISTLE THE EIGHTH.

TO MY FRIEND, MR J. NORTHLEIGH, AUTHOR OF THE PARALLEL; ON HIS TRIUMPH OF THE BRITISH MONARCHY.

So Joseph, yet a youth, expounded well
The boding dream, and did the event foretell;
Judged by the past, and drew the Parallel.
Thus early Solomon the truth explored,
The right awarded, and the babe restored.
Thus Daniel, ere to prophecy he grew,

The perjured Presbyters did first subdue,
And freed Susanna from the canting crew.
Well may our monarchy triumphant stand,
While warlike James protects both sea and land;
And, under covert of his seven-fold shield,
Thou send'st thy shafts to scour the distant field.
By law thy powerful pen has set us free;
Thou studiest that, and that may study thee.

EPISTLE THE NINTH.

TO SIR GEORGE ETHEREGE.

To you, who live in chill degree,
As map informs, of fifty-three,
And do not much for cold atone,
By bringing thither fifty-one,
Methinks all climes should be alike,
From tropic even to pole artique;
Since you have such a constitution
As no where suffers diminution.
You can be old in grave debate,
And young in love affairs of state;
And both to wives and husbands show
The vigour of a plenipo.
Like mighty missioner you come
Ad Partes Infidelium.
A work of wonderous merit sure,
So far to go, so much t'endure;
And all to preach to German dame,
Where sound of Cupid never came.
Less had you done, had you been sent
As far as Drake or Pinto went,
For cloves or nutmegs to the line-a,
Or even for oranges to China.
That had indeed been charity,
Where love-sick ladies helpless lie,
Chapt, and, for want of liquor, dry.
But you have made your zeal appear
Within the circle of the Bear.
What region of the earth's so dull,
That is not of your labours full?
Triptolemus (so sung the Nine)
Strewed plenty from his cart divine;
But spite of all these fable-makers,
He never sowed on Almain acres.

No, that was left by fate's decree
To be performed and sung by thee.
Thou break'st through forms with as much ease
As the French king through articles.
In grand affairs thy days are spent,
In waging weighty compliment,
With such as monarchs represent.
They, whom such vast fatigues attend,
Want some soft minutes to unbend,
To shew the world that, now and then,
Great ministers are mortal men.
Then Rhenish rummers walk the round;
In bumpers every king is crowned;
Besides three holy mitred Hectors,
And the whole college of Electors.
No health of potentate is sunk,
That pays to make his envoy drunk.
These Dutch delights, I mentioned last,
Suit not, I know, your English taste:
For wine to leave a whore or play,
Was ne'er your Excellency's way.
Nor need this title give offence,
For here you were your Excellence;
For gaming, writing, speaking, keeping,
His Excellence for all—but sleeping.
Now if you tope in form, and treat,
'Tis the sour sauce to the sweet meat,
The fine you pay for being great.
Nay, here's a harder imposition,
Which is indeed the court's petition,
That, setting worldly pomp aside,
Which poet has at font denied,
You would be pleased in humble way
To write a trifle called a Play.
This truly is a degradation,
But would oblige the crown and nation
Next to your wise negotiation.
If you pretend, as well you may,
Your high degree, your friends will say,
The duke St Aignon made a play.
If Gallic wit convince you scarce,
His grace of Bucks has made a farce,
And you, whose comic wit is terse all,
Can hardly fall below Rehearsal.
Then finish what you have began,
But scribble faster if you can;
For yet no George, to our discerning,
Has writ without a ten years warning.

EPISTLE THE TENTH.

TO MR SOUTHERNE, ON HIS COMEDY CALLED THE WIVES' EXCUSE, ACTED IN 1692.

Sure there's a fate in plays, and 'tis in vain
To write, while these malignant planets reign.
Some very foolish influence rules the pit,
Not always kind to sense, or just to wit;
And whilst it lasts, let buffoonry succeed,
To make us laugh, for never was more need.
Farce, in itself, is of a nasty scent;
But the gain smells not of the excrement.
The Spanish nymph, a wit and beauty too,
With all her charms, bore but a single show;
But let a monster Muscovite appear,
He draws a crowded audience round the year.
May be thou hast not pleased the box and pit;
Yet those who blame thy tale applaud thy wit:
So Terence plotted, but so Terence writ.
Like his, thy thoughts are true, thy language clean;
Even lewdness is made moral in thy scene.
The hearers may for want of Nokes repine;
But rest secure, the readers will be thine.
Nor was thy laboured drama damned or hissed,
But with a kind civility dismissed;
With such good manners as the Wife did use,
Who, not accepting, did but just refuse.
There was a glance at parting; such a look,
As bids thee not give o'er for one rebuke.
But if thou wouldst be seen, as well as read,
Copy one living author, and one dead.
The standard of thy style let Etherege be;
For wit, the immortal spring of Wycherly.
Learn, after both, to draw some just design,
And the next age will learn to copy thine.

EPISTLE THE ELEVENTH.

TO HENRY HIGDEN, ESQ. ON HIS TRANSLATION OF THE TENTH SATIRE OF JUVENAL.

The Grecian wits, who satire first began,
Were pleasant Pasquins on the life of man;
At mighty villains, who the state opprest,

They durst not rail, perhaps; they lashed, at least,
And turned them out of office with a jest.
No fool could peep abroad, but ready stand
The drolls to clap a bauble in his hand.
Wise legislators never yet could draw
A fop within the reach of common law;
For posture, dress, grimace, and affectation,
Though foes to sense, are harmless to the nation.
Our last redress is dint of verse to try,
And satire is our court of chancery.
This way took Horace to reform an age,
Not bad enough to need an author's rage:
But yours, who lived in more degenerate times,
Was forced to fasten deep, and worry crimes.
Yet you, my friend, have tempered him so well,
You make him smile in spite of all his zeal;
An art peculiar to yourself alone,
To join the virtues of two styles in one.
Oh! were your author's principle received,
Half of the labouring world would be relieved;
For not to wish is not to be deceived.
Revenge would into charity be changed,
Because it costs too dear to be revenged;
It costs our quiet and content of mind,
And when 'tis compassed leaves a sting behind.
Suppose I had the better end o'the staff,
Why should I help the ill-natured world to laugh?
'Tis all alike to them, who get the day;
They love the spite and mischief of the fray.
No; I have cured myself of that disease;
Nor will I be provoked, but when I please:
But let me half that cure to you restore;
You give the salve, I laid it to the sore.
Our kind relief against a rainy day,
Beyond a tavern, or a tedious play,
We take your book, and laugh our spleen away.
If all your tribe, too studious of debate,
Would cease false hopes and titles to create,
Led by the rare example you begun,
Clients would fail, and lawyers be undone.

EPISTLE THE TWELFTH.

TO MY DEAR FRIEND MR CONGREVE, ON HIS COMEDY CALLED THE DOUBLE DEALER.

Well, then, the promised hour is come at last,

The present age of wit obscures the past:
Strong were our sires, and as they fought they writ,
Conquering with force of arms, and dint of wit:
Theirs was the giant race, before the flood;
And thus, when Charles returned, our empire stood.
Like Janus, he the stubborn soil manured,
With rules of husbandry the rankness cured;
Tamed us to manners when the stage was rude,
And boisterous English wit with art endued.
Our age was cultivated thus at length;
But what we gained in skill we lost in strength.
Our builders were with want of genius curst;
The second temple was not like the first;
Till you, the best Vitruvius, come at length,
Our beauties equal, but excel our strength.
Firm Doric pillars found your solid base;
The fair Corinthian crowns the higher space:
Thus all below is strength, and all above is grace.
In easy dialogue is Fletcher's praise;
He moved the mind, but had not power to raise:
Great Jonson did by strength of judgment please;
Yet, doubling Fletcher's force, he wants his ease.
In differing talents both adorned their age;
One for the study, t'other for the stage.
But both to Congreve justly shall submit,
One matched in judgment, both o'ermatched in wit.
In him all beauties of this age we see,
Etherege his courtship, Southerne's purity,
The satire, wit, and strength, of manly Wycherly.
All this in blooming youth you have atchieved;
Nor are your foiled contemporaries grieved.
So much the sweetness of your manners move,
We cannot envy you, because we love.
Fabius might joy in Scipio, when he saw
A beardless consul made against the law,
And join his suffrage to the votes of Rome,
Though he with Hannibal was overcome.
Thus old Romano bowed to Raphael's fame,
And scholar to the youth he taught became.
O that your brows my laurel had sustained!
Well had I been deposed, if you had reigned:
The father had descended for the son;
For only you are lineal to the throne.
Thus, when the state one Edward did depose,
A greater Edward in his room arose:
But now not I, but poetry, is cursed;
For Tom the second reigns like Tom the first.
But let them not mistake my patron's part,

Nor call his charity their own desert.
Yet this I prophecy,—Thou shalt be seen,
(Though with some short parenthesis between,)
High on the throne of wit, and, seated there,
Not mine,—that's little,—but thy laurel wear.
Thy first attempt an early promise made;
That early promise this has more than paid.
So bold, yet so judiciously you dare,
That your least praise is to be regular.
Time, place, and action, may with pains be wrought,
But genius must be born, and never can be taught.
This is your portion, this your native store;
Heaven, that but once was prodigal before,
To Shakespeare gave as much,—she could not give him more.
Maintain your post; that's all the fame you need;
For 'tis impossible you should proceed.
Already I am worn with cares and age,
And just abandoning the ungrateful stage;
Unprofitably kept at heaven's expence,
I live a rent-charge on his providence:
But you, whom every muse and grace adorn,
Whom I foresee to better fortune born,
Be kind to my remains; and O defend,
Against your judgment, your departed friend!
Let not the insulting foe my fame pursue,
But shade those laurels which descend to you:
And take for tribute what these lines express;
You merit more, nor could my love do less.

EPISTLE THE THIRTEENTH.

TO MR GRANVILLE, ON HIS EXCELLENT TRAGEDY, CALLED HEROIC LOVE.

Auspicious poet, wert thou not my friend,
How could I envy, what I must commend!
But since 'tis nature's law, in love and wit,
That youth should reign, and withering age submit,
With less regret those laurels I resign,
Which, dying on my brows, revive on thine.
With better grace an ancient chief may yield
The long contended honours of the field,
Than venture all his fortune at a cast,
And fight, like Hannibal, to lose at last.
Young princes, obstinate to win the prize,
Though yearly beaten, yearly yet they rise:
Old monarchs, though successful, still in doubt,

Catch at a peace, and wisely turn devout.
Thine be the laurel, then; thy blooming age
Can best, if any can, support the stage;
Which so declines, that shortly we may see
Players and plays reduced to second infancy:
Sharp to the world, but thoughtless of renown,
They plot not on the stage, but on the town,
And, in despair their empty pit to fill,
Set up some foreign monster in a bill.
Thus they jog on, still tricking, never thriving,
And murdering plays, which they miscal reviving.
Our sense is nonsense, through their pipes conveyed;
Scarce can a poet know the play he made,
'Tis so disguised in death; nor thinks 'tis he
That suffers in the mangled tragedy.
Thus Itys first was killed, and after dressed
For his own sire, the chief invited guest.
I say not this of thy successful scenes,
Where thine was all the glory, theirs the gains.
With length of time, much judgment, and more toil,
Not ill they acted what they could not spoil.
Their setting-sun still shoots a glimmering ray,
Like ancient Rome, majestic in decay;
And better gleanings their worn soil can boast,
Than the crab-vintage of the neighbouring coast.
This difference yet the judging world will see;
Thou copiest Homer, and they copy thee.

EPISTLE THE FOURTEENTH.

TO MY FRIEND MR MOTTEUX, ON HIS TRAGEDY CALLED BEAUTY IN DISTRESS, PUBLISHED IN 1698.

'Tis hard, my friend, to write in such an age,
As damns not only poets, but the stage.
That sacred art, by heaven itself infused,
Which Moses, David, Solomon, have used,
Is now to be no more: the Muses' foes
Would sink their Maker's praises into prose.
Were they content to prune the lavish vine
Of straggling branches, and improve the wine,
Who, but a madman, would his thoughts defend?
All would submit; for all but fools will mend.
But when to common sense they give the lie,
And turn distorted words to blasphemy,
They give the scandal; and the wise discern,
Their glosses teach an age, too apt to learn.

What I have loosely, or prophanely, writ,
Let them to fires, their due desert, commit:
Nor, when accused by me, let them complain;
Their faults, and not their function, I arraign.
Rebellion, worse than witchcraft, they pursued;
The pulpit preached the crime, the people rued.
The stage was silenced; for the saints would see
In fields performed their plotted tragedy.
But let us first reform, and then so live,
That we may teach our teachers to forgive;
Our desk be placed below their lofty chairs,
Ours be the practice, as the precept theirs.
The moral part, at least we may divide,
Humility reward, and punish pride;
Ambition, interest, avarice, accuse;
These are the province of a tragic muse.
These hast thou chosen; and the public voice
Has equalled thy performance with thy choice.
Time, action, place, are so preserved by thee,
That e'en Corneille might with envy see
The alliance of his tripled unity.
Thy incidents, perhaps, too thick are sown,
But too much plenty is thy fault alone.
At least but two can that good crime commit,
Thou in design, and Wycherly in wit.
Let thy own Gauls condemn thee, if they dare,
Contented to be thinly regular:
Born there, but not for them, our fruitful soil
With more increase rewards thy happy toil.
Their tongue, enfeebled, is refined too much,
And, like pure gold, it bends at every touch.
Our sturdy Teuton yet will art obey,
More fit for manly thought, and strengthened with allay.
But whence art thou inspired, and thou alone,
To flourish in an idiom not thy own?
It moves our wonder, that a foreign guest
Should overmatch the most, and match the best.
In under-praising thy deserts, I wrong;
Here find the first deficience of our tongue:
Words, once my stock, are wanting, to commend
So great a poet, and so good a friend.

EPISTLE THE FIFTEENTH.

TO MY HONOURED KINSMAN JOHN DRIDEN, OF CHESTERTON, IN THE COUNTY OF HUNTINGDON, ESQ.

How blessed is he, who leads a country life,
Unvexed with anxious cares, and void of strife!
Who, studying peace, and shunning civil rage,
Enjoyed his youth, and now enjoys his age:
All who deserve his love, he makes his own;
And, to be loved himself, needs only to be known.
Just, good, and wise, contending neighbours come,
From your award to wait their final doom;
And, foes before, return in friendship home.
Without their cost, you terminate the cause,
And save the expence of long litigious laws;
Where suits are traversed, and so little won,
That he who conquers is but last undone:
Such are not your decrees; but so designed,
The sanction leaves a lasting peace behind;
Like your own soul, serene, a pattern of your mind.
Promoting concord, and composing strife,
Lord of yourself, uncumbered with a wife;
Where, for a year, a month, perhaps a night,
Long penitence succeeds a short delight:
Minds are so hardly matched, that even the first,
Though paired by heaven, in Paradise were cursed.
For man and woman, though in one they grow,
Yet, first or last, return again to two.
He to God's image, she to his was made;
So, farther from the fount the stream at random strayed.
How could he stand, when, put to double pain,
He must a weaker than himself sustain!
Each might have stood perhaps, but each alone;
Two wrestlers help to pull each other down.
Not that my verse would blemish all the fair;
But yet if some be bad, 'tis wisdom to beware,
And better shun the bait, than struggle in the snare.
Thus have you shunned, and shun the married state,
Trusting as little as you can to fate.
No porter guards the passage of your door,
To admit the wealthy, and exclude the poor;
For God, who gave the riches, gave the heart,
To sanctify the whole, by giving part;
Heaven, who foresaw the will, the means has wrought,
And to the second son a blessing brought;
The first-begotten had his father's share;
But you, like Jacob, are Rebecca's heir.
So may your stores and fruitful fields increase;
And ever be you blessed, who live to bless.
As Ceres sowed, where-e'er her chariot flew;
As heaven in deserts rained the bread of dew;

So free to many, to relations most,
You feed with manna your own Israel host.
With crowds attended of your ancient race,
You seek the champaign sports, or sylvan chace;
With well-breathed beagles you surround the wood,
Even then industrious of the common good;
And often have you brought the wily fox
To suffer for the firstlings of the flocks;
Chased even amid the folds, and made to bleed,
Like felons, where they did the murderous deed.
This fiery game your active youth maintained;
Not yet by years extinguished, though restrained:
You season still with sports your serious hours;
For age but tastes of pleasures, youth devours.
The hare in pastures or in plains is found,
Emblem of human life; who runs the round,
And, after all his wandering ways are done,
His circle fills, and ends where he begun,
Just as the setting meets the rising sun.
Thus princes ease their cares; but happier he,
Who seeks not pleasure through necessity,
Than such as once on slippery thrones were placed,
And chasing, sigh to think themselves are chased.
So lived our sires, ere doctors learned to kill,
And multiplied with theirs the weekly bill.
The first physicians by debauch were made;
Excess began, and sloth sustains the trade.
Pity the generous kind their cares bestow
To search forbidden truths, (a sin to know,)
To which if human science could attain,
The doom of death, pronounced by God, were vain.
In vain the leech would interpose delay;
Fate fastens first, and vindicates the prey.
What help from art's endeavours can we have?
Guibbons but guesses, nor is sure to save;
But Maurus sweeps whole parishes, and peoples every grave;
And no more mercy to mankind will use,
Than when he robbed and murdered Maro's muse.
Would'st thou be soon dispatched, and perish whole,
Trust Maurus with thy life, and Milbourne with thy soul.
By chace our long-lived fathers earned their food;
Toil strung the nerves, and purified the blood:
But we their sons, a pampered race of men,
Are dwindled down to threescore years and ten.
Better to hunt in fields, for health unbought,
Than fee the doctor for a nauseous draught.
The wise, for care, on exercise depend;
God never made his work for man to mend.

The tree of knowledge, once in Eden placed,
Was easy found, but was forbid the taste:
O had our grandsire walked without his wife,
He first had sought the better plant of life!
Now both are lost: yet, wandering in the dark,
Physicians, for the tree, have found the bark;
They, labouring for relief of human kind,
With sharpened sight some remedies may find;
The apothecary-train is wholly blind.
From files a random recipe they take,
And many deaths of one prescription make.
Garth, generous as his muse, prescribes and gives;
The shopman sells, and by destruction lives:
Ungrateful tribe! who, like the viper's brood,
From Med'cine issuing, suck their mother's blood!
Let these obey, and let the learned prescribe,
That men may die without a double bribe;
Let them, but under their superiors, kill,
When doctors first have signed the bloody bill;
He 'scapes the best, who, nature to repair,
Draws physic from the fields, in draughts of vital air.
You hoard not health for your own private use,
But on the public spend the rich produce.
When, often urged, unwilling to be great,
Your country calls you from your loved retreat,
And sends to senates, charged with common care,
Which none more shuns, and none can better bear:
Where could they find another formed so fit,
To poise, with solid sense, a sprightly wit?
Were these both wanting, as they both abound,
Where could so firm integrity be found?
Well born, and wealthy, wanting no support,
You steer betwixt the country and the court;
Nor gratify whate'er the great desire,
Nor grudging give, what public needs require.
Part must be left, a fund when foes invade,
And part employed to roll the watery trade;
Even Canaan's happy land, when worn with toil,
Required a sabbath-year to mend the meagre soil.
Good senators (and such as you) so give,
That kings may be supplied, the people thrive:
And he, when want requires, is truly wise,
Who slights not foreign aids, nor overbuys,
But on our native strength, in time of need, relies.
Munster was bought, we boast not the success;
Who fights for gain, for greater makes his peace.
Our foes, compelled by need, have peace embraced;
The peace both parties want, is like to last;

Which if secure, securely we may trade;
Or, not secure, should never have been made.
Safe in ourselves, while on ourselves we stand,
The sea is ours, and that defends the land.
Be, then, the naval stores the nation's care,
New ships to build, and battered to repair.
Observe the war, in every annual course;
What has been done, was done with British force:
Namur subdued, is England's palm alone;
The rest besieged, but we constrained the town:
We saw the event that followed our success;
France, though pretending arms, pursued the peace,
Obliged, by one sole treaty, to restore
What twenty years of war had won before.
Enough for Europe has our Albion fought;
Let us enjoy the peace our blood has bought.
When once the Persian king was put to flight,
The weary Macedons refused to fight;
Themselves their own mortality confessed,
And left the son of Jove to quarrel for the rest.
Even victors are by victories undone;
Thus Hannibal, with foreign laurels won,
To Carthage was recalled, too late to keep his own.
While sore of battle, while our wounds are green,
Why should we tempt the doubtful dye again?
In wars renewed, uncertain of success;
Sure of a share, as umpires of the peace.
A patriot both the king and country serves;
Prerogative and privilege preserves:
Of each our laws the certain limit show;
One must not ebb, nor t'other overflow:
Betwixt the prince and parliament we stand,
The barriers of the state on either hand;
May neither overflow, for then they drown the land.
When both are full, they feed our blessed abode;
Like those that watered once the paradise of God.
Some overpoise of sway, by turns, they share;
In peace the people, and the prince in war:
Consuls of moderate power in calms were made;
When the Gauls came, one sole dictator swayed.
Patriots, in peace, assert the people's right,
With noble stubbornness resisting might;
No lawless mandates from the court receive,
Nor lend by force, but in a body give.
Such was your generous grandsire; free to grant
In parliaments, that weighed their prince's want:
But so tenacious of the common cause,
As not to lend the king against his laws;

And, in a loathsome dungeon doomed to lie,
In bonds retained his birthright liberty,
And shamed oppression, till it set him free.
O true descendant of a patriot line,
Who, while thou shar'st their lustre, lend'st them thine.
Vouchsafe this picture of thy soul to see;
'Tis so far good, as it resembles thee;
The beauties to the original I owe,
Which when I miss, my own defects I show:
Nor think the kindred muses thy disgrace;
A poet is not born in every race.
Two of a house few ages can afford,
One to perform, another to record.
Praise-worthy actions are by thee embraced,
And 'tis my praise to make thy praises last.
For even when death dissolves our human frame,
The soul returns to heaven from whence it came;
Earth keeps the body, verse preserves the fame.

EPISTLE THE SIXTEENTH.

TO SIR GODFREY KNELLER. PRINCIPAL PAINTER TO HIS MAJESTY.

Once I beheld the fairest of her kind,
And still the sweet idea charms my mind:
True, she was dumb; for nature gazed so long,
Pleased with her work, that she forgot her tongue;
But, smiling, said—She still shall gain the prize;
I only have transferred it to her eyes.
Such are thy pictures, Kneller, such thy skill,
That nature seems obedient to thy will;
Comes out, and meets thy pencil in the draught,
Lives there, and wants but words to speak her thought.
At least thy pictures look a voice; and we
Imagine sounds, deceived to that degree,
We think 'tis somewhat more than just to see.
Shadows are but privations of the light;
Yet, when we walk, they shoot before the sight;
With us approach, retire, arise, and fall;
Nothing themselves, and yet expressing all.
Such are thy pieces, imitating life
So near, they almost conquer in the strife;
And from their animated canvas came,
Demanding souls, and loosened from the frame.
Prometheus, were he here, would cast away
His Adam, and refuse a soul to clay;

And either would thy noble work inspire,
Or think it warm enough, without his fire.
But vulgar hands may vulgar likeness raise;
This is the least attendant on thy praise:
From hence the rudiments of art began;
A coal, or chalk, first imitated man:
Perhaps the shadow, taken on a wall,
Gave outlines to the rude original;
Ere canvas yet was strained, before the grace
Of blended colours found their use and place,
Or cypress tablets first received a face.
By slow degrees the godlike art advanced;
As man grew polished, picture was enhanced:
Greece added posture, shade, and perspective,
And then the mimic piece began to live.
Yet perspective was lame, no distance true,
But all came forward in one common view:
No point of light was known, no bounds of art;
When light was there, it knew not to depart,
But glaring on remoter objects played;
Not languished and insensibly decayed.
Rome raised not art, but barely kept alive,
And with old Greece unequally did strive;
Till Goths and Vandals, a rude northern race,
Did all the matchless monuments deface.
Then all the Muses in one ruin lie,
And rhyme began to enervate poetry.
Thus, in a stupid military state,
The pen and pencil find an equal fate.
Flat faces, such as would disgrace a skreen,
Such as in Bantam's embassy were seen,
Unraised, unrounded, were the rude delight
Of brutal nations, only born to fight.
Long time the sister arts, in iron sleep,
A heavy sabbath did supinely keep;
At length, in Raphael's age, at once they rise,
Stretch all their limbs, and open all their eyes.
Thence rose the Roman, and the Lombard line;
One coloured best, and one did best design.
Raphael's, like Homer's, was the nobler part,
But Titian's painting looked like Virgil's art.
Thy genius gives thee both; where true design,
Postures unforced, and lively colours join,
Likeness is ever there; but still the best,
(Like proper thoughts in lofty language drest,)
Where light, to shades descending, plays, not strives,
Dies by degrees, and by degrees revives.
Of various parts a perfect whole is wrought;

Thy pictures think, and we divine their thought.
Shakespeare, thy gift, I place before my sight;
With awe, I ask his blessing ere I write;
With reverence look on his majestic face;
Proud to be less, but of his godlike race.
His soul inspires me, while thy praise I write,
And I, like Teucer, under Ajax fight;
Bids thee, through me, be bold; with dauntless breast
Contemn the bad, and emulate the best.
Like his, thy critics in the attempt are lost;
When most they rail, know then, they envy most.
In vain they snarl aloof; a noisy crowd,
Like women's anger, impotent and loud.
While they their barren industry deplore,
Pass on secure, and mind the goal before,
Old as she is, my muse shall march behind,
Bear off the blast, and intercept the wind.
Our arts are sisters, though not twins in birth,
For hymns were sung in Eden's happy earth:
But oh, the painter muse, though last in place,
Has seized the blessing first, like Jacob's race.
Apelles' art an Alexander found,
And Raphael did with Leo's gold abound;
But Homer was with barren laurel crowned.
Thou hadst thy Charles a while, and so had I;
But pass we that unpleasing image by.
Rich in thyself, and of thyself divine,
All pilgrims come and offer at thy shrine.
A graceful truth thy pencil can command;
The fair themselves go mended from thy hand.
Likeness appears in every lineament,
But likeness in thy work is eloquent.
Though nature there her true resemblance bears,
A nobler beauty in thy piece appears.
So warm thy work, so glows the generous frame,
Flesh looks less living in the lovely dame.
Thou paint'st as we describe, improving still,
When on wild nature we ingraft our skill,
Yet not creating beauties at our will.
But poets are confined in narrower space,
To speak the language of their native place;
The painter widely stretches his command,
Thy pencil speaks the tongue of every land.
From hence, my friend, all climates are your own,
Nor can you forfeit, for you hold of none.
All nations all immunities will give
To make you theirs, where'er you please to live;
And not seven cities, but the world, would strive.

Sure some propitious planet then did smile,
When first you were conducted to this isle;
Our genius brought you here, to enlarge our fame,
For your good stars are every where the same.
Thy matchless hand, of every region free,
Adopts our climate, not our climate thee.
Great Rome and Venice early did impart
To thee the examples of their wonderous art.
Those masters, then but seen, not understood,
With generous emulation fired thy blood;
For what in nature's dawn the child admired,
The youth endeavoured, and the man acquired.
If yet thou hast not reached their high degree,
'Tis only wanting to this age, not thee.
Thy genius, bounded by the times, like mine,
Drudges on petty draughts, nor dare design
A more exalted work, and more divine.
For what a song, or senseless opera,
Is to the living labour of a play;
Or what a play to Virgil's work would be,
Such is a single piece to history.
But we, who life bestow, ourselves must live;
Kings cannot reign, unless their subjects give;
And they, who pay the taxes, bear the rule:
Thus thou, sometimes, art forced to draw a fool;
But so his follies in thy posture sink,
The senseless idiot seems at last to think.
Good heaven! that sots and knaves should be so vain,
To wish their vile resemblance may remain,
And stand recorded, at their own request,
To future days, a libel or a jest!
Else should we see your noble pencil trace
Our unities of action, time, and place;
A whole composed of parts, and those the best,
With every various character exprest;
Heroes at large, and at a nearer view;
Less, and at distance, an ignoble crew;
While all the figures in one action join,
As tending to complete the main design.
More cannot be by mortal art exprest,
But venerable age shall add the rest:
For time shall with his ready pencil stand,
Retouch your figures with his ripening hand,
Mellow your colours, and imbrown the teint,
Add every grace, which time alone can grant;
To future ages shall your fame convey,
And give more beauties than he takes away.

ELEGIES AND EPITAPHS.

UPON THE DEATH OF LORD HASTINGS.

Must noble Hastings immaturely die,
The honour of his ancient family,
Beauty and learning thus together meet,
To bring a winding for a wedding-sheet?
Must virtue prove death's harbinger? must she,
With him expiring, feel mortality?
Is death, sin's wages, grace's now? shall art
Make us more learned, only to depart?
If merit be disease; if virtue, death;
To be good, not to be; who'd then bequeath
Himself to discipline? who'd not esteem
Labour a crime? study self-murder deem?
Our noble youth now have pretence to be
Dunces securely, ignorant healthfully.
Rare linguist, whose worth speaks itself, whose praise,
Though not his own, all tongues besides do raise:
Than whom great Alexander may seem less,
Who conquered men, but not their languages.
In his mouth nations spake; his tongue might be
Interpreter to Greece, France, Italy.
His native soil was the four parts o'the earth;
All Europe was too narrow for his birth.
A young apostle; and,—with reverence may
I speak't,—inspired with gift of tongues, as they.
Nature gave him, a child, what men in vain
Oft strive, by art though furthered, to obtain.
His body was an orb, his sublime soul
Did move on virtue's and on learning's pole;
Whose regular motions better to our view,
Than Archimedes' sphere, the heavens did shew.
Graces and virtues, languages and arts,
Beauty and learning, filled up all the parts.
Heaven's gifts, which do like falling stars appear
Scattered in others, all, as in their sphere,
Were fixed, conglobate in his soul, and thence
Shone through his body, with sweet influence;
Letting their glories so on each limb fall,
The whole frame rendered was celestial.
Come, learned Ptolemy, and trial make,
If thou this hero's altitude can'st take:
But that transcends thy skill; thrice happy all,
Could we but prove thus astronomical.

Lived Tycho now, struck with this ray which shone
More bright i'the morn, than others beam at noon,
He'd take his astrolabe, and seek out here
What new star 'twas did gild our hemisphere.
Replenished then with such rare gifts as these,
Where was room left for such a foul disease?
The nation's sin hath drawn that veil, which shrouds
Our day-spring in so sad benighting clouds.
Heaven would no longer trust its pledge, but thus
Recalled it,—rapt its Ganymede from us.
Was there no milder way but the small-pox,
The very filthiness of Pandora's box?
So many spots, like næves on Venus' soil,
One jewel set off with so many a foil;
Blisters with pride swelled, which through's flesh did sprout
Like rose-buds, stuck i'the lily-skin about.
Each little pimple had a tear in it,
To wail the fault its rising did commit;
Which, rebel-like, with its own lord at strife,
Thus made an insurrection 'gainst his life.
Or were these gems sent to adorn his skin,
The cabinet of a richer soul within?
No comet need foretel his change drew on,
Whose corpse might seem a constellation.
O had he died of old, how great a strife
Had been, who from his death should draw their life;
Who should, by one rich draught, become whate'er
Seneca, Cato, Numa, Cæsar, were!
Learned, virtuous, pious, great; and have by this
An universal metempsychosis.
Must all these aged sires in one funeral
Expire? all die in one so young, so small?
Who, had he lived his life out, his great fame
Had swoln 'bove any Greek or Roman name.
But hasty winter, with one blast, hath brought
The hopes of autumn, summer, spring, to nought.
Thus fades the oak i'the sprig, i'the blade the corn;
Thus without young, this Phœnix dies, new-born.
Must then old three-legged grey-beards with their gout,
Catarrhs, rheums, aches, live three ages out?
Time's offals, only fit for the hospital!
Or to hang antiquaries rooms withal!
Must drunkards, lechers, spent with sinning, live
With such helps as broths, possets, physic give?
None live, but such as should die? shall we meet
With none but ghostly fathers in the street?
Grief makes me rail, sorrow will force its way,
And showers of tears tempestuous sighs best lay.

The tongue may fail; but overflowing eyes
Will weep out lasting streams of elegies.
But thou, O virgin-widow, left alone,
Now thy beloved, heaven-ravished spouse is gone,
Whose skilful sire in vain strove to apply
Med'cines, when thy balm was no remedy;
With greater than Platonic love, O wed
His soul, though not his body, to thy bed:
Let that make thee a mother; bring thou forth
The ideas of his virtue, knowledge, worth;
Transcribe the original in new copies; give
Hastings o'the better part: so shall he live
In's nobler half; and the great grandsire be
Of an heroic divine progeny:
An issue which to eternity shall last,
Yet but the irradiations which he cast.
Erect no mausoleums; for his best
Monument is his spouse's marble breast.

TO THE MEMORY OF MR OLDHAM.

Farewell, too little, and too lately known,
Whom I began to think, and call my own:
For sure our souls were near allied, and thine
Cast in the same poetic mould with mine.
One common note on either lyre did strike,
And knaves and fools we both abhorred alike.
To the same goal did both our studies drive;
The last set out, the soonest did arrive.
Thus Nisus fell upon the slippery place,
Whilst his young friend performed and won the race.
O early ripe! to thy abundant store
What could advancing age have added more!
It might (what nature never gives the young)
Have taught the numbers of thy native tongue.
But satire needs not those, and wit will shine
Through the harsh cadence of a rugged line.
A noble error, and but seldom made,
When poets are by too much force betrayed.
Thy generous fruits, though gathered ere their prime,
Still shewed a quickness; and maturing time
But mellows what we write, to the dull sweets of rhyme.
Once more, hail, and farewell! farewell, thou young,
But ah too short, Marcellus of our tongue!
Thy brows with ivy, and with laurels bound;
But fate and gloomy night encompass thee around.

TO THE PIOUS MEMORY OF THE ACCOMPLISHED YOUNG LADY MRS ANNE KILLIGREW, EXCELLENT IN THE TWO SISTER ARTS OF POESY AND PAINTING.

AN ODE.

I.
Thou youngest virgin-daughter of the skies,
Made in the last promotion of the blest;
Whose palms, new plucked from paradise,
In spreading branches more sublimely rise,
Rich with immortal green above the rest:
Whether, adopted to some neighbouring star,
Thou roll'st above us, in thy wandering race,
Or, in procession fixed and regular,
Mov'st with the heaven's majestic pace;
Or, called to more superior bliss,
Thou tread'st with seraphims the vast abyss:
Whatever happy region is thy place,
Cease thy celestial song a little space;
Thou wilt have time enough for hymns divine,
Since heaven's eternal year is thine.
Hear, then, a mortal muse thy praise rehearse,
In no ignoble verse;
But such as thy own voice did practise here,
When thy first fruits of poesy were given,
To make thyself a welcome inmate there;
While yet a young probationer,
And candidate of heaven.

II.
If by traduction came thy mind,
Our wonder is the less to find
A soul so charming from a stock so good;
Thy father was transfused into thy blood:
So wert thou born into a tuneful strain,
An early, rich, and inexhausted vein.
But if thy pre-existing soul
Was formed, at first, with myriads more,
It did through all the mighty poets roll,
Who Greek or Latin laurels wore,
And was that Sappho last, which once it was before.
If so, then cease thy flight, O heaven-born mind!
Thou hast no dross to purge from thy rich ore:
Nor can thy soul a fairer mansion find,
Than was the beauteous frame she left behind:

Return to fill or mend the choir of thy celestial kind.

III.
May we presume to say, that, at thy birth,
New joy was sprung in heaven, as well as here on earth.
For sure the milder planets did combine
On thy auspicious horoscope to shine,
And e'en the most malicious were in trine.
Thy brother-angels at thy birth
Strung each his lyre, and tuned it high,
That all the people of the sky
Might know a poetess was born on earth;
And then, if ever, mortal ears
Had heard the music of the spheres.
And if no clustering swarm of bees
On thy sweet mouth distilled their golden dew,
'Twas that such vulgar miracles
Heaven had not leisure to renew:
For all thy blest fraternity of love
Solemnized there thy birth, and kept thy holiday above.

IV.
O gracious God! how far have we
Prophaned thy heavenly gift of poesy?
Made prostitute and profligate the muse,
Debased to each obscene and impious use,
Whose harmony was first ordained above
For tongues of angels, and for hymns of love?
O wretched we! why were we hurried down
This lubrique and adulterate age,
(Nay, added fat pollutions of our own)
T'increase the streaming ordures of the stage?
What can we say t'excuse our second fall?
Let this thy vestal, heaven, atone for all:
Her Arethusian stream remains unsoiled,
Unmixed with foreign filth, and undefiled;
Her wit was more than man, her innocence a child.

V.
Art she had none, yet wanted none;
For nature did that want supply:
So rich in treasures of her own,
She might our boasted stores defy:
Such noble vigour did her verse adorn,
That it seemed borrowed where 'twas only born.
Her morals, too, were in her bosom bred,
By great examples daily fed,
What in the best of books, her father's life, she read:

And to be read herself she need not fear;
Each test, and every light, her muse will bear,
Though Epictetus with his lamp were there.
E'en love (for love sometimes her muse exprest)
Was but a lambent flame which played about her breast:
Light as the vapours of a morning dream,
So cold herself, whilst she such warmth exprest,
'Twas Cupid bathing in Diana's stream.

VI.
Born to the spacious empire of the Nine,
One would have thought she should have been content
To manage well that mighty government;
But what can young ambitious souls confine?
To the next realm she stretched her sway,
For Painture near adjoining lay,
A plenteous province, and alluring prey.
A chamber of dependencies was framed,
(As conquerors will never want pretence,
When armed, to justify the offence,)
And the whole fief, in right of poetry, she claimed.
The country open lay without defence;
For poets frequent inroads there had made,
And perfectly could represent
The shape, the face, with every lineament,
And all the large domains which the Dumb Sister swayed;
All bowed beneath her government,
Received in triumph wheresoe'er she went.
Her pencil drew whate'er her soul designed,
And oft the happy draught surpassed the image in her mind.
The sylvan scenes of herds and flocks,
And fruitful plains and barren rocks,
Of shallow brooks that flowed so clear,
The bottom did the top appear;
Of deeper too and ampler floods,
Which, as in mirrors, shewed the woods;
Of lofty trees, with sacred shades,
And perspectives of pleasant glades,
Where nymphs of brightest form appear,
And shaggy satyrs standing near,
Which them at once admire and fear.
The ruins too of some majestic piece,
Boasting the power of ancient Rome or Greece,
Whose statues, frizes, columns, broken lie,
And, though defaced, the wonder of the eye;
What nature, art, bold fiction, e'er durst frame,
Her forming hand gave feature to the name.
So strange a concourse ne'er was seen before,

But when the peopled ark the whole creation bore.

VII.
The scene then changed; with bold erected look
Our martial king the sight with reverence strook:
For, not content to express his outward part,
Her hand called out the image of his heart:
His warlike mind, his soul devoid of fear,
His high-designing thoughts were figured there,
As when, by magic, ghosts are made appear.
Our phœnix queen was pourtrayed too so bright,
Beauty alone could beauty take so right:
Her dress, her shape, her matchless grace,
Were all observed, as well as heavenly face.
With such a peerless majesty she stands,
As in that day she took the crown from sacred hands:
Before a train of heroines was seen,
In beauty foremost, as in rank, the queen.
Thus nothing to her genius was denied,
But like a ball of fire the further thrown,
Still with a greater blaze she shone,
And her bright soul broke out on every side.
What next she had designed, heaven only knows:
To such immoderate growth her conquest rose,
That fate alone its progress could oppose.

VIII.
Now all those charms, that blooming grace,
The well-proportioned shape, and beauteous face,
Shall never more be seen by mortal eyes;
In earth the much-lamented virgin lies.
Not wit, nor piety, could fate prevent;
Nor was the cruel destiny content
To finish all the murder at a blow,
To sweep at once her life and beauty too;
But, like a hardened felon, took a pride
To work more mischievously slow,
And plundered first, and then destroyed.
O double sacrilege on things divine,
To rob the relic, and deface the shrine!
But thus Orinda died;
Heaven, by the same disease, did both translate;
As equal were their souls, so equal was their fate.

IX.
Meantime, her warlike brother on the seas
His waving streamers to the winds displays,
And vows for his return, with vain devotion, pays.

Ah, generous youth! that wish forbear,
The winds too soon will waft thee here:
Slack all thy sails, and fear to come;
Alas, thou know'st not, thou art wrecked at home!
No more shalt thou behold thy sister's face,
Thou hast already had her last embrace.
But look aloft, and if thou ken'st from far
Among the Pleiads a new-kindled star,
If any sparkles than the rest more bright,
Tis she that shines in that propitious light.

X.
When in mid-air the golden trump shall sound,
To raise the nations under ground;
When in the valley of Jehosophat,
The judging God shall close the book of fate,
And there the last assizes keep,
For those who wake, and those who sleep;
When rattling bones together fly,
From the four corners of the sky;
When sinews o'er the skeletons are spread,
Those clothed with flesh, and life inspires the dead;
The sacred poets first shall hear the sound,
And foremost from the tomb shall bound,
For they are covered with the lightest ground;
And straight, with inborn vigour, on the wing,
Like mounting larks, to the new morning sing.
There thou, sweet saint, before the choir shall go,
As harbinger of heaven, the way to show,
The way which thou so well hast learnt below.

UPON THE DEATH OF THE VISCOUNT OF DUNDEE.

Oh last and best of Scots! who didst maintain
Thy country's freedom from a foreign reign;
New people fill the land now thou art gone,
New gods the temples, and new kings the throne.
Scotland and thou did each in other live;
Nor would'st thou her, nor could she thee survive.
Farewell! who, dying, didst support the state,
And couldst not fall but with thy country's fate.

ELEONORA: A PANEGYRICAL POEM, DEDICATED TO THE MEMORY OF THE LATE COUNTESS OF ABINGDON.

—Superas evadere per auras,
Hoc opus, hic labor est. Pauci quos æquus amavit
Jupiter, aut ardens evixit ad æthera virtus,
Diis geniti potuere.
VIRGIL. Æneid. lib. vi.

TO THE RIGHT HONOURABLE THE EARL OF ABINGDON, &c.

MY LORD,

The commands, with which you honoured me some months ago, are now performed: they had been sooner, but betwixt ill health, some business, and many troubles, I was forced to defer them till this time. Ovid, going to his banishment, and writing from on shipboard to his friends, excused the faults of his poetry by his misfortunes; and told them, that good verses never flow, but from a serene and composed spirit. Wit, which is a kind of Mercury, with wings fastened to his head and heels, can fly but slowly in a damp air. I therefore chose rather to obey you late than ill: if at least I am capable of writing any thing, at any time, which is worthy your perusal and your patronage. I cannot say that I have escaped from a shipwreck; but have only gained a rock by hard swimming, where I may pant awhile and gather breath; for the doctors give me a sad assurance, that my disease never took its leave of any man, but with a purpose to return. However, my lord, I have laid hold on the interval, and managed the small stock, which age has left me, to the best advantage, in performing this inconsiderable service to my lady's memory. We, who are priests of Apollo, have not the inspiration when we please; but must wait till the God comes rushing on us, and invades us with a fury which we are not able to resist; which gives us double strength while the fit continues, and leaves us languishing and spent, at its departure. Let me not seem to boast, my lord, for I have really felt it on this occasion, and prophesied beyond my natural power. Let me add, and hope to be believed, that the excellency of the subject contributed much to the happiness of the execution; and that the weight of thirty years was taken off me while I was writing. I swam with the tide, and the water under me was buoyant. The reader will easily observe, that I was transported by the multitude and variety of my similitudes; which are generally the product of a luxuriant fancy, and the wantonness of wit. Had I called in my judgment to my assistance, I had certainly retrenched many of them. But I defend them not; let them pass for beautiful faults amongst the better sort of critics; for the whole poem, though written in that which they call heroic verse, is of the pindaric nature, as well in the thought as the expression; and, as such, requires the same grains of allowance for it. It was intended, as your lordship sees in the title, not for an elegy, but a panegyric: a kind of apotheosis, indeed, if a heathen word may be applied to a Christian use. And on all occasions of praise, if we take the ancients for our patterns, we are bound by prescription to employ the magnificence of words, and the force of figures, to adorn the sublimity of thoughts. Isocrates amongst the Grecian orators, and Cicero, and the younger Pliny, amongst the Romans, have left us their precedents for our security; for I think I need not mention the inimitable Pindar, who stretches on these pinions out of sight, and is carried upward, as it were, into another world.

This, at least, my lord, I may justly plead, that, if I have not performed so well as I think I have, yet I have used my best endeavours to excel myself. One disadvantage I have had, which is, never to have known or seen my lady; and to draw the lineaments of her mind from the description which I have received from others, is for a painter to set himself at work without the living original before him; which, the more beautiful it is, will be so much the more difficult for him to conceive, when he has only a relation given him of such and such features by an acquaintance or a friend, without the nice touches, which give the best resemblance, and make the graces of the picture. Every artist is apt enough to flatter himself, and I amongst the rest, that their own ocular observations would have discovered more perfections, at least others, than have been delivered to them; though I have received mine from the best hands, that is, from persons who neither want a just understanding of my lady's worth, nor a due veneration for her memory.

Doctor Donne, the greatest wit, though not the best poet of our nation, acknowledges, that he had never seen Mrs Drury, whom he has made immortal in his admirable "Anniversaries." I have had the same fortune, though I have not succeeded to the same genius. However, I have followed his footsteps in the design of his panegyric; which was to raise an emulation in the living, to copy out the example of the dead. And therefore it was, that I once intended to have called this poem "The Pattern;" and though, on a second consideration, I changed the title into the name of that illustrious person, yet the design continues, and Eleonora is still the pattern of charity, devotion, and humility; of the best wife, the best mother, and the best of friends.

And now, my lord, though I have endeavoured to answer your commands, yet I could not answer it to the world, nor to my conscience, if I gave not your lordship my testimony of being the best husband now living: I say my testimony only; for the praise of it is given you by yourself. They, who despise the rules of virtue both in their practice and their morals, will think this a very trivial commendation. But I think it the peculiar happiness of the Countess of Abingdon, to have been so truly loved by you, while she was living, and so gratefully honoured, after she was dead. Few there are who have either had, or could have, such a loss; and yet fewer, who carried their love and constancy beyond the grave. The exteriors of mourning, a decent funeral, and black habits, are the usual stints of common husbands; and perhaps their wives deserve no better than to be mourned with hypocrisy, and forgot with ease. But you have distinguished yourself from ordinary lovers, by a real and lasting grief for the deceased; and by endeavouring to raise for her the most durable monument, which is that of verse. And so it would have proved, if the workman had been equal to the work, and your choice of the artificer as happy as your design. Yet, as Phidias, when he had made the statue of Minerva, could not forbear to engrave his own name, as author of the piece; so give me leave to hope, that, by subscribing mine to this poem, I may live by the goddess, and transmit my name to posterity by the memory of hers. It is no flattery to assure your lordship, that she is remembered, in the present age, by all who have had the honour of her conversation and acquaintance; and that I have never been in any company since the news of her death was first brought me, where they have not extolled her virtues, and even spoken the same things of her in prose, which I have done in verse.

I therefore think myself obliged to your lordship for the commission which you have given me: how I have acquitted myself of it, must be left to the opinion of the world, in spite of any protestation which I can enter against the present age, as incompetent or corrupt judges. For my comfort, they are but Englishmen; and, as such, if they think ill of me to-day, they are inconstant enough to think well of me to-morrow. And after all, I have not much to thank my fortune that I was born amongst them. The good of both sexes are so few, in England, that they stand like exceptions against general rules; and though one of them has deserved a greater commendation than I could give her, they have taken care that I should not tire my pen with frequent exercise on the like subjects; that praises, like taxes, should be appropriated, and left almost as individual as the person. They say, my talent is satire; if it be so, it is a fruitful age, and there is an extraordinary crop to gather, but a single hand is insufficient for such a harvest: they have sown the dragon's teeth themselves, and it is but just they should reap each other in lampoons. You, my lord, who have the character of honour, though it is not my happiness to know you, may stand aside, with the small remainders of the English nobility, truly such, and, unhurt yourselves, behold the mad combat. If I have pleased you, and some few others, I have obtained my end. You see I have disabled myself, like an elected Speaker of the House; yet, like him, I have undertaken the charge, and find the burden sufficiently recompensed by the honour. Be pleased to accept of these my unworthy labours, this paper monument; and let her pious memory, which I am sure is sacred to you, not only plead the pardon of my many faults, but gain me your protection, which is ambitiously sought by,

My LORD,
Your Lordship's
Most obedient servant,
JOHN DRYDEN.

ELEONORA: A PANEGYRICAL POEM, DEDICATED TO THE MEMORY OF THE LATE COUNTESS OF ABINGDON.

ARGUMENT.

From the Marginal Notes of the First Edition.

The introduction. Of her charity. Of her prudent management. Of her humility. Of her piety. Of her various virtues. Of her conjugal virtues. Of her love to her children. Her care of their education. Of her friendship. Reflections on the shortness of her life. The manner of her death. Her preparedness to die. Apostrophe to her soul. Epiphonema, or close of the poem.

As when some great and gracious monarch dies,
Soft whispers first, and mournful murmurs, rise
Among the sad attendants; then the sound
Soon gathers voice, and spreads the news around,
Through town and country, till the dreadful blast
Is blown to distant colonies at last,
Who then, perhaps, were offering vows in vain,
For his long life, and for his happy reign:
So slowly, by degrees, unwilling fame
Did matchless Eleonora's fate proclaim,
Till public as the loss the news became.
The nation felt it in the extremest parts,
With eyes o'erflowing, and with bleeding hearts;
But most the poor, whom daily she supplied,
Beginning to be such, but when she died.
For, while she lived, they slept in peace by night,
Secure of bread, as of returning light,
And with such firm dependence on the day,
That need grew pampered, and forgot to pray;
So sure the dole, so ready at their call,
They stood prepared to see the manna fall.

Such multitudes she fed, she clothed, she nurst,
That she herself might fear her wanting first.
Of her five talents, other five she made;
Heaven, that had largely given, was largely paid;
And in few lives, in wonderous few, we find
A fortune better fitted to the mind.
Nor did her alms from ostentation fall,
Or proud desire of praise—the soul gave all:
Unbribed it gave; or, if a bribe appear,
No less than heaven, to heap huge treasures there.
Want passed for merit at her open door:
Heaven saw, he safely might increase his poor,
And trust their sustenance with her so well,
As not to be at charge of miracle.
None could be needy, whom she saw or knew;
All in the compass of her sphere she drew:
He, who could touch her garment, was as sure,
As the first Christians of the apostles' cure.
The distant heard, by fame, her pious deeds,
And laid her up for their extremest needs;
A future cordial for a fainting mind;
For, what was ne'er refused, all hoped to find,
Each in his turn: the rich might freely come,
As to a friend; but to the poor, 'twas home.
As to some holy house the afflicted came,
The hunger-starved, the naked, and the lame,
Want and diseases fled before her name.
For zeal like her's her servants were too slow;
She was the first, where need required, to go;
Herself the foundress and attendant too.
Sure she had guests sometimes to entertain,
Guests in disguise, of her great Master's train:
Her Lord himself might come, for aught we know,
Since in a servant's form he lived below:
Beneath her roof he might be pleased to stay;
Or some benighted angel, in his way,
Might ease his wings, and, seeing heaven appear
In its best work of mercy, think it there;
Where all the deeds of charity and love
Were in as constant method, as above,
All carried on; all of a piece with theirs;
As free her alms, as diligent her cares;
As loud her praises, and as warm her prayers.
Yet was she not profuse; but feared to waste,
And wisely managed, that the stock might last;
That all might be supplied, and she not grieve,
When crowds appeared, she had not to relieve:
Which to prevent, she still increased her store;

Laid up, and spared, that she might give the more.
So Pharaoh, or some greater king than he,
Provided for the seventh necessity;
Taught from above his magazines to frame,
That famine was prevented ere it came.
Thus heaven, though all-sufficient, shews a thrift
In his œconomy, and bounds his gift;
Creating for our day one single light,
And his reflection too supplies the night.
Perhaps a thousand other worlds, that lie
Remote from us, and latent in the sky,
Are lightened by his beams, and kindly nurst,
Of which our earthly dunghill is the worst.
Now, as all virtues keep the middle line,
Yet somewhat more to one extreme incline,
Such was her soul; abhorring avarice,
Bounteous, but almost bounteous to a vice;
Had she given more, it had profusion been,
And turned the excess of goodness into sin.
These virtues raised her fabric to the sky;
For that which is next heaven is charity.
But as high turrets for their airy steep
Require foundations in proportion deep,
And lofty cedars as far upward shoot
As to the nether heavens they drive the root;
So low did her secure foundation lie,
She was not humble, but humility.
Scarcely she knew that she was great, or fair,
Or wise, beyond what other women are,
Or, which is better, knew, but never durst compare.
For, to be conscious of what all admire,
And not be vain, advances virtue higher.
But still she found, or rather thought she found,
Her own worth wanting, others' to abound;
Ascribed above their due to every one,
Unjust and scanty to herself alone.
Such her devotion was, as might give rules
Of speculation to disputing schools,
And teach us equally the scales to hold
Betwixt the two extremes of hot and cold;
That pious heat may moderately prevail,
And we be warmed, but not be scorched with zeal.
Business might shorten, not disturb, her prayer;
Heaven had the best, if not the greater share.
An active life long orisons forbids;
Yet still she prayed, for still she prayed by deeds.
Her every day was sabbath; only free
From hours of prayer, for hours of charity.

Such as the Jews from servile toil released,
Where works of mercy were a part of rest;
Such as blest angels exercise above,
Varied with sacred hymns and acts of love;
Such sabbaths as that one she now enjoys,
E'en that perpetual one, which she employs,
(For such vicissitudes in heaven there are)
In praise alternate, and alternate prayer.
All this she practised here, that when she sprung
Amidst the choirs, at the first sight she sung;
Sung, and was sung herself in angels' lays;
For, praising her, they did her Maker praise.
All offices of heaven so well she knew,
Before she came, that nothing there was new;
And she was so familiarly received,
As one returning, not as one arrived.
Muse, down again precipitate thy flight;
For how can mortal eyes sustain immortal light?
But as the sun in water we can bear,
Yet not the sun, but his reflection there,
So let us view her here in what she was,
And take her image in this watery glass:
Yet look not every lineament to see;
Some will be cast in shades, and some will be
So lamely drawn, you'll scarcely know 'tis she.
For where such various virtues we recite,
'Tis like the milky-way, all over bright,
But sown so thick with stars, 'tis undistinguished light.
Her virtue, not her virtues, let us call;
For one heroic comprehends them all:
One, as a constellation is but one,
Though 'tis a train of stars, that, rolling on,
Rise in their turn, and in the zodiac run,
Ever in motion; now 'tis faith ascends,
Now hope, now charity, that upward tends,
And downwards with diffusive good descends.
As in perfumes composed with art and cost,
Tis hard to say what scent is uppermost;
Nor this part musk or civet can we call,
Or amber, but a rich result of all;
So she was all a sweet, whose every part,
In due proportion mixed, proclaimed the Maker's art.
No single virtue we could most commend,
Whether the wife, the mother, or the friend;
For she was all, in that supreme degree,
That as no one prevailed, so all was she.
The several parts lay hidden in the piece;
The occasion but exerted that, or this.

A wife as tender, and as true withal,
As the first woman was before her fall:
Made for the man, of whom she was a part;
Made to attract his eyes, and keep his heart.
A second Eve, but by no crime accurst;
As beauteous, not as brittle as the first.
Had she been first, still Paradise had been,
And death had found no entrance by her sin.
So she not only had preserved from ill
Her sex and ours, but lived their pattern still.
Love and obedience to her lord she bore;
She much obeyed him, but she loved him more:
Not awed to duty by superior sway,
But taught by his indulgence to obey.
Thus we love God, as author of our good;
So subjects love just kings, or so they should.
Nor was it with ingratitude returned;
In equal fires the blissful couple burned;
One joy possessed them both, and in one grief they mourned.
His passion still improved; he loved so fast,
As if he feared each day would be her last.
Too true a prophet to foresee the fate
That should so soon divide their happy state;
When he to heaven entirely must restore
That love, that heart, where he went halves before.
Yet as the soul is all in every part,
So God and he might each have all her heart.
So had her children too; for charity
Was not more fruitful, or more kind, than she:
Each under other by degrees they grew;
A goodly perspective of distant view.
Anchises looked not with so pleased a face,
In numbering o'er his future Roman race,
And marshalling the heroes of his name,
As, in their order, next to light they came;
Nor Cybele, with half so kind an eye,
Surveyed her sons and daughters of the sky;
Proud, shall I say, of her immortal fruit?
As far as pride with heavenly minds may suit.
Her pious love excelled to all she bore;
New objects only multiplied it more.
And as the chosen found the pearly grain
As much as every vessel could contain;
As in the blissful vision each shall share
As much of glory as his soul can bear;
So did she love, and so dispense her care.
Her eldest thus, by consequence, was best,
As longer cultivated than the rest.

The babe had all that infant care beguiles,
And early knew his mother in her smiles:
But when dilated organs let in day
To the young soul, and gave it room to play,
At his first aptness, the maternal love
Those rudiments of reason did improve:
The tender age was pliant to command;
Like wax it yielded to the forming hand:
True to the artificer, the laboured mind
With ease was pious, generous, just, and kind;
Soft for impression, from the first prepared,
Till virtue with long exercise grew hard:
With every act confirmed, and made at last
So durable as not to be effaced,
It turned to habit; and, from vices free,
Goodness resolved into necessity.
Thus fixed she virtue's image, (that's her own,)
Till the whole mother in the children shone;
For that was their perfection: she was such,
They never could express her mind too much.
So unexhausted her perfections were,
That, for more children, she had more to spare;
For souls unborn, whom her untimely death
Deprived of bodies, and of mortal breath;
And, could they take the impressions of her mind,
Enough still left to sanctify her kind.
Then wonder not to see this soul extend
The bounds, and seek some other self, a friend;
As swelling seas to gentle rivers glide,
To seek repose, and empty out the tide;
So this full soul, in narrow limits pent,
Unable to contain her, sought a vent
To issue out, and in some friendly breast
Discharge her treasures, and securely rest;
To unbosom all the secrets of her heart,
Take good advice, but better to impart.
For 'tis the bliss of friendship's holy state,
To mix their minds, and to communicate;
Though bodies cannot, souls can penetrate:
Fixed to her choice, inviolably true,
And wisely choosing, for she chose but few.
Some she must have; but in no one could find
A tally fitted for so large a mind.
The souls of friends like kings in progress are,
Still in their own, though from the palace far:
Thus her friend's heart her country dwelling was,
A sweet retirement to a coarser place;
Where pomp and ceremonies entered not,

Where greatness was shut out, and business well forgot.
This is the imperfect draught; but short as far
As the true height and bigness of a star
Exceeds the measures of the astronomer.
She shines above, we know; but in what place,
How near the throne, and heaven's imperial face,
By our weak optics is but vainly guessed;
Distance and altitude conceal the rest.
Though all these rare endowments of the mind
Were in a narrow space of life confined,
The figure was with full perfection crowned;
Though not so large an orb, as truly round.
As when in glory, through the public place,
The spoils of conquered nations were to pass,
And but one day for triumph was allowed,
The consul was constrained his pomp to crowd;
And so the swift procession hurried on,
That all, though not distinctly, might be shewn:
So in the straitened bounds of life confined,
She gave but glimpses of her glorious mind;
And multitudes of virtues passed along,
Each pressing foremost in the mighty throng,
Ambitious to be seen, and then make room
For greater multitudes that were to come.
Yet unemployed no minute slipped away;
Moments were precious in so short a stay.
The haste of heaven to have her was so great,
That some were single acts, though each complete;
But every act stood ready to repeat.
Her fellow-saints with busy care will look
For her blest name in fate's eternal book;
And, pleased to be outdone, with joy will see
Numberless virtues, endless charity:
But more will wonder at so short an age,
To find a blank beyond the thirtieth page;
And with a pious fear begin to doubt
The piece imperfect, and the rest torn out.
But 'twas her Saviour's time; and, could there be
A copy near the original, 'twas she.
As precious gums are not for lasting fire,
They but perfume the temple, and expire;
So was she soon exhaled, and vanished hence;
A short sweet odour, of a vast expence.
She vanished, we can scarcely say she died;
For but a now did heaven and earth divide:
She passed serenely with a single breath;
This moment perfect health, the next was death:
One sigh did her eternal bliss assure;

So little penance needs, when souls are almost pure.
As gentle dreams our waking thoughts pursue,
Or, one dream passed, we slide into a new;
So close they follow, such wild order keep,
We think ourselves awake, and are asleep;
So softly death succeeded life in her,
She did but dream of heaven, and she was there.
No pains she suffered, nor expired with noise;
Her soul was whispered out with God's still voice;
As an old friend is beckoned to a feast,
And treated like a long-familiar guest.
He took her as he found, but found her so,
As one in hourly readiness to go;
E'en on that day, in all her trim prepared,
As early notice she from heaven had heard,
And some descending courier from above
Had given her timely warning to remove;
Or counselled her to dress the nuptial room,
For on that night the bridegroom was to come.
He kept his hour, and found her where she lay,
Clothed all in white, the livery of the day:
Scarce had she sinned in thought, or word, or act,
Unless omissions were to pass for fact;
That hardly death a consequence could draw,
To make her liable to nature's law.
And, that she died, we only have to shew
The mortal part of her she left below;
The rest, so smooth, so suddenly she went,
Looked like translation through the firmament,
Or like the fiery car on the third errand sent.
O happy soul! if thou canst view from high,
Where thou art all intelligence, all eye,
If looking up to God, or down to us,
Thou find'st, that any way be pervious,
Survey the ruins of thy house, and see
Thy widowed and thy orphan family;
Look on thy tender pledges left behind;
And, if thou canst a vacant minute find
From heavenly joys, that interval afford
To thy sad children, and thy mourning lord.
See how they grieve, mistaken in their love,
And shed a beam of comfort from above;
Give them, as much as mortal eyes can bear,
A transient view of thy full glories there;
That they with moderate sorrow may sustain,
And mollify their losses in thy gain.
Or else divide the grief; for such thou wert,
That should not all relations bear a part,

It were enough to break a single heart.
Let this suffice: nor thou, great saint, refuse
This humble tribute, of no vulgar muse;
Who, not by cares, or wants, or age deprest,
Stems a wild deluge with a dauntless breast;
And dares to sing thy praises in a clime
Where vice triumphs, and virtue is a crime;
Where e'en to draw the picture of thy mind,
Is satire on the most of human kind:
Take it, while yet 'tis praise; before my rage,
Unsafely just, break loose on this bad age;
So bad, that thou thyself hadst no defence
From vice, but barely by departing hence.
Be what, and where thou art; to wish thy place,
Were, in the best, presumption more than grace.
Thy relics, (such thy works of mercy are)
Have, in this poem, been my holy care.
As earth thy body keeps, thy soul the sky,
So shall this verse preserve thy memory;
For thou shalt make it live, because it sings of thee.

ON THE DEATH OF AMYNTAS. A PASTORAL ELEGY.

'Twas on a joyless and a gloomy morn,
Wet was the grass, and hung with pearls the thorn,
When Damon, who designed to pass the day
With hounds and horns, and chace the flying prey,
Rose early from his bed; but soon he found
The welkin pitched with sullen clouds around,
An eastern wind, and dew upon the ground.
Thus while he stood, and sighing did survey
The fields, and curst the ill omens of the day,
He saw Menalcas come with heavy pace:
Wet were his eyes, and cheerless was his face:
He wrung his hands, distracted with his care,
And sent his voice before him from afar.
"Return," he cried, "return, unhappy swain,
The spungy clouds are filled with gathering rain:
The promise of the day not only crossed,
But even the spring, the spring itself is lost.
Amyntas—oh!"—he could not speak the rest,
Nor needed, for presaging Damon guessed.
Equal with heaven young Damon loved the boy,
The boast of nature, both his parents' joy.
His graceful form revolving in his mind;
So great a genius, and a soul so kind,

Gave sad assurance that his fears were true;
Too well the envy of the gods he knew:
For when their gifts too lavishly are placed,
Soon they repent, and will not make them last.
For sure it was too bountiful a dole,
The mother's features, and the father's soul.
Then thus he cried:—"The morn bespoke the news;
The morning did her cheerful light diffuse;
But see how suddenly she changed her face,
And brought on clouds and rain, the day's disgrace;
Just such, Amyntas, was thy promised race.
What charms adorned thy youth, where nature smiled,
And more than man was given us in a child!
His infancy was ripe; a soul sublime
In years so tender that prevented time:
Heaven gave him all at once; then snatched away,
Ere mortals all his beauties could survey;
Just like the flower that buds and withers in a day.

MENALCAS.
The mother, lovely, though with grief opprest,
Reclined his dying head upon her breast.
The mournful family stood all around;
One groan was heard, one universal sound:
All were in floods of tears and endless sorrow drowned.
So dire a sadness sat on every look,
Even death repented he had given the stroke.
He grieved his fatal work had been ordained,
But promised length of life to those who yet remained.
The mother's and her eldest daughter's grace,
It seems, had bribed him to prolong their space.
The father bore it with undaunted soul,
Like one who durst his destiny controul;
Yet with becoming grief he bore his part,
Resigned his son, but not resigned his heart.
Patient as Job; and may he live to see,
Like him, a new increasing family!

DAMON.
Such is my wish, and such my prophecy;
For yet, my friend, the beauteous mould remains;
Long may she exercise her fruitful pains!
But, ah! with better hap, and bring a race
More lasting, and endued with equal grace!
Equal she may, but farther none can go;
For he was all that was exact below.

MENALCAS.
Damon, behold yon breaking purple cloud;
Hear'st thou not hymns and songs divinely loud?
There mounts Amyntas; the young cherubs play
About their godlike mate, and sing him on his way.
He cleaves the liquid air; behold, he flies,
And every moment gains upon the skies.
The new-come guest admires the ethereal state,
The sapphire portal, and the golden gate;
And now admitted in the shining throng,
He shows the passport which he brought along.
His passport is his innocence and grace,
Well known to all the natives of the place.
Now sing, ye joyful angels, and admire
Your brother's voice that comes to mend your quire:
Sing you, while endless tears our eyes bestow;
For, like Amyntas, none is left below.

ON THE DEATH OF A VERY YOUNG GENTLEMAN.

He, who could view the book of destiny,
And read whatever there was writ of thee,
O charming youth, in the first opening page,
So many graces in so green an age,
Such wit, such modesty, such strength of mind,
A soul at once so manly and so kind,
Would wonder when he turned the volume o'er,
And, after some few leaves, should find no more.
Nought but a blank remain, a dead void space,
A step of life that promised such a race.
We must not, dare not, think, that heaven began
A child, and could not finish him a man;
Reflecting what a mighty store was laid
Of rich materials, and a model made:
The cost already furnished; so bestowed,
As more was never to one soul allowed:
Yet after this profusion spent in vain,
Nothing but mouldering ashes to remain,
I guess not, lest I split upon the shelf,
Yet, durst I guess, heaven kept it for himself;
And giving us the use, did soon recal,
Ere we could spare the mighty principal.
Thus then he disappeared, was rarefied,
For 'tis improper speech to say he died:
He was exhaled; his great Creator drew

His spirit, as the sun the morning dew.
'Tis sin produces death; and he had none,
But the taint Adam left on every son.
He added not, he was so pure, so good,
'Twas but the original forfeit of his blood;
And that so little, that the river ran
More clear than the corrupted fount began.
Nothing remained of the first muddy clay;
The length of course had washed it in the way:
So deep, and yet so clear, we might behold
The gravel bottom, and that bottom gold.
As such we loved, admired, almost adored,
Gave all the tribute mortals could afford.
Perhaps we gave so much, the powers above
Grew angry at our superstitious love;
For when we more than human homage pay,
The charming cause is justly snatched away.
Thus was the crime not his, but ours alone;
And yet we murmur that he went so soon,
Though miracles are short, and rarely shown.
Learn then, ye mournful parents, and divide
That love in many, which in one was tied.
That individual blessing is no more,
But multiplied in your remaining store.
The flame's dispersed, but does not all expire;
The sparkles blaze, though not the globe of fire.
Love him by parts, in all your numerous race,
And from those parts form one collected grace;
Then, when you have refined to that degree,
Imagine all in one, and think that one is he.

UPON YOUNG MR ROGERS, OF GLOUCESTERSHIRE.

Of gentle blood, his parents only treasure,
Their lasting sorrow, and their vanished pleasure.
Adorned with features, virtues, wit, and grace,
A large provision for so short a race:
More moderate gifts might have prolonged his date,
Too early fitted for a better state:
But, knowing heaven his home, to shun delay,
He leaped o'er age, and took the shortest way.

ON THE DEATH OF MR PURCELL.

SET TO MUSIC BY DR BLOW.

I.
Mark how the lark and linnet sing,
With rival notes
They strain their warbling throats,
To welcome in the spring.
But in the close of night,
When Philomel begins her heavenly lay,
They cease their mutual spite,
Drink in her music with delight,
And, listening, silently obey.

II.
So ceased the rival crew when Purcell came;
They sung no more, or only sung his fame.
Struck dumb, they all admired the godlike man:
The godlike man,
Alas! too soon retired,
As he too late began.
We beg not hell our Orpheus to restore;
Had he been there,
Their sovereign's fear
Had sent him back before.
The power of harmony too well they knew:
He long ere this had tuned their jarring sphere,
And left no hell below.

III.
The heavenly choir, who heard his notes from high,
Let down the scale of music from the sky;
They handed him along,
And all the way he taught, and all the way they sung.
Ye brethren of the lyre, and tuneful voice,
Lament his lot, but at your own rejoice:
Now live secure, and linger out your days;
The gods are pleased alone with Purcell's lays,
Nor know to mend their choice.

EPITAPH ON THE LADY WHITMORE.

Fair, kind, and true, a treasure each alone,
A wife, a mistress, and a friend, in one;
Rest in this tomb, raised at thy husband's cost,
Here sadly summing, what he had, and lost.
Come, virgins, ere in equal bands ye join,

Come first and offer at her sacred shrine;
Pray but for half the virtues of this wife,
Compound for all the rest, with longer life;
And wish your vows, like hers, may be returned,
So loved when living, and, when dead, so mourned.

EPITAPH ON MRS MARGARET PASTON, OF BURNINGHAM, IN NORFOLK.

So fair, so young, so innocent, so sweet,
So ripe a judgment, and so rare a wit,
Require at least an age in one to meet.
In her they met; but long they could not stay,
'Twas gold too fine to mix without allay.
Heaven's image was in her so well exprest,
Her very sight upbraided all the rest;
Too justly ravished from an age like this,
Now she is gone, the world is of a piece.

EPITAPH ON THE MONUMENT OF THE MARQUIS OF WINCHESTER.

He who, in impious times, undaunted stood,
And 'midst rebellion durst be just and good;
Whose arms asserted, and whose sufferings more
Confirmed the cause for which he fought before,
Rests here, rewarded by an heavenly prince,
For what his earthly could not recompence.
Pray, reader, that such times no more appear;
Or, if they happen, learn true honour here.
Ask of this age's faith and loyalty,
Which, to preserve them, heaven confined in thee.
Few subjects could a king like thine deserve;
And fewer, such a king so well could serve.
Blest king, blest subject, whose exalted state
By sufferings rose, and gave the law to fate!
Such souls are rare, but mighty patterns given
To earth, and meant for ornaments to heaven.

EPITAPH ON SIR PALMES FAIRBONE'S TOMB IN WESTMINSTER-ABBEY.

Ye sacred relics, which your marble keep,
Here, undisturbed by wars, in quiet sleep;
Discharge the trust, which, when it was below,

Fairbone's undaunted soul did undergo,
And be the town's palladium from the foe.
Alive and dead these walls he will defend:
Great actions great examples must attend.
The Candian siege his early valour knew,
Where Turkish blood did his young hands imbrue.
From thence returning with deserved applause,
Against the Moors his well-fleshed sword he draws;
The same the courage, and the same the cause.
His youth and age, his life and death, combine,
As in some great and regular design,
All of a piece throughout, and all divine.
Still nearer heaven his virtues shone more bright,
Like rising flames expanding in their height;
The martyr's glory crowned the soldier's fight.
More bravely British general never fell,
Nor general's death was e'er revenged so well;
Which his pleased eyes beheld before their close,
Followed by thousand victims of his foes.
To his lamented loss, for time to come,
His pious widow consecrates this tomb.

ON THE MONUMENT OF A FAIR MAIDEN LADY, WHO DIED AT BATH, AND IS THERE INTERRED.

Below this marble monument is laid
All that heaven wants of this celestial maid.
Preserve, O sacred tomb, thy trust consigned;
The mold was made on purpose for the mind:
And she would lose, if, at the latter day,
One atom could be mixed of other clay;
Such were the features of her heavenly face,
Her limbs were formed with such harmonious grace:
So faultless was the frame, as if the whole
Had been an emanation of the soul;
Which her own inward symmetry revealed,
And like a picture shone, in glass annealed;
Or like the sun eclipsed, with shaded light;
Too piercing, else, to be sustained by sight.
Each thought was visible that rolled within;
As through a crystal case the figured hours are seen.
And heaven did this transparent veil provide,
Because she had no guilty thought to hide.
All white, a virgin-saint, she sought the skies,
For marriage, though it sullies not, it dyes.
High though her wit, yet humble was her mind;
As if she could not, or she would not find

How much her worth transcended all her kind.
Yet she had learned so much of heaven below,
That when arrived, she scarce had more to know;
But only to refresh the former hint,
And read her Maker in a fairer print.
So pious, as she had no time to spare
For human thoughts, but was confined to prayer;
Yet in such charities she passed the day,
'Twas wondrous how she found an hour to pray.
A soul so calm, it knew not ebbs or flows,
Which passion could but curl, not discompose.
A female softness, with a manly mind;
A daughter duteous, and a sister kind;
In sickness patient, and in death resigned.

UNDER MR MILTON'S PICTURE, BEFORE HIS PARADISE LOST.

Three poets, in three distant ages born,
Greece, Italy, and England, did adorn.
The first, in loftiness of thought surpassed;
The next, in majesty; in both, the last.
The force of nature could no further go;
To make a third, she joined the former two.

PASTORALS

PASTORAL I.

OR, TITYRUS AND MELIBOEUS.

ARGUMENT.

The occasion of the First Pastoral was this: When Augustus had settled himself in the Roman empire, that he might reward his veteran troops for their past service, he distributed among them all the lands that lay about Cremona and Mantua; turning out the right owners for having sided with his enemies. Virgil was a sufferer among the rest, who afterwards recovered his estate by Mæcenas's intercession; and, as an instance of his gratitude, composed the following Pastoral, where he sets out his own good fortune in the person of Tityrus, and the calamities of his Mantuan neighbours in the character of Meliboeus.

MELIBOEUS
Beneath the shade which beechen boughs diffuse,
You, Tityrus, entertain your sylvan muse.
Round the wide world in banishment we roam,

Forced from our pleasing fields and native home;
While, stretched at ease, you sing your happy loves,
And Amaryllis fills the shady groves.

TITYRUS
These blessings, friend, a deity bestowed;
For never can I deem him less than God.
The tender firstlings of my woolly breed
Shall on his holy altar often bleed.
He gave my kine to graze the flowery plain,
And to my pipe renewed the rural strain.

MELIBOEUS
I envy not your fortune, but admire,
That, while the raging sword and wasteful fire
Destroy the wretched neighbourhood around,
No hostile arms approach your happy ground.
Far different is my fate; my feeble goats
With pains I drive from their forsaken cotes:
And this, you see, I scarcely drag along,
Who, yeaning, on the rocks has left her young,
The hope and promise of my failing fold.
My loss, by dire portents, the gods foretold;
For, had I not been blind, I might have seen:—
Yon riven oak, the fairest of the green,
And the hoarse raven, on the blasted bough,
By croaking from the left, presaged the coming blow.
But tell me, Tityrus, what heavenly power
Preserved your fortunes in that fatal hour?

TITYRUS
Fool that I was, I thought imperial Rome
Like Mantua, where on market-days we come,
And thither drive our tender lambs from home.
So kids and whelps their sires and dams express,
And so the great I measured by the less.
But country towns, compared with her, appear
Like shrubs, when lofty cypresses are near.

MELIBOEUS
What great occasion called you hence to Rome?

TITYRUS
Freedom, which came at length, though slow to come.
Nor did my search of liberty begin,
Till my black hairs were changed upon my chin;
Nor Amaryllis would vouchsafe a look,
Till Galatea's meaner bonds I broke.

Till then a helpless, hopeless, homely swain,
I sought not freedom, nor aspired to gain:
Though many a victim from my folds was bought,
And many a cheese to country markets brought,
Yet all the little that I got, I spent,
And still returned as empty as I went.

MELIBOEUS
We stood amazed to see your mistress mourn,
Unknowing that she pined for your return;
We wondered why she kept her fruit so long,
For whom so late the ungathered apples hung.
But now the wonder ceases, since I see
She kept them only, Tityrus, for thee;
For thee the bubbling springs appeared to mourn,
And whispering pines made vows for thy return.

TITYRUS
What should I do?—While here I was enchained,
No glimpse of godlike liberty remained;
Nor could I hope, in any place but there,
To find a god so present to my prayer.
There first the youth of heavenly birth I viewed,
For whom our monthly victims are renewed.
He heard my vows, and graciously decreed
My grounds to be restored, my former flocks to feed.

MELIBOEUS
O fortunate old man! whose farm remains—
For you sufficient—and requites your pains;
Though rushes overspread the neighbouring plains,
Though here the marshy grounds approach your fields,
And there the soil a stony harvest yields.
Your teeming ewes shall no strange meadows try,
Nor fear a rot from tainted company.
Behold! yon bordering fence of sallow trees
Is fraught with flowers, the flowers are fraught with bees;
The busy bees, with a soft murmuring strain,
Invite to gentle sleep the labouring swain.
While, from the neighbouring rock, with rural songs,
The pruner's voice the pleasing dream prolongs,
Stock-doves and turtles tell their amorous pain,
And, from the lofty elms, of love complain.

TITYRUS
The inhabitants of seas and skies shall change,
And fish on shore, and stags in air, shall range,
The banished Parthian dwell on Arar's brink,

And the blue German shall the Tigris drink,
Ere I, forsaking gratitude and truth,
Forget the figure of that godlike youth.

MELIBOEUS
But we must beg our bread in climes unknown,
Beneath the scorching or the freezing zone;
And some to far Oaxis shall be sold,
Or try the Libyan heat, or Scythian cold;
The rest among the Britons be confined,
A race of men from all the world disjoined.
O! must the wretched exiles ever mourn,
Nor, after length of rolling years, return?
Are we condemned by fate's unjust decree,
No more our houses and our homes to see?
Or shall we mount again the rural throne,
And rule the country kingdoms, once our own?
Did we for these barbarians plant and sow?
On these, on these, our happy fields bestow?
Good heaven! what dire effects from civil discord flow!
Now let me graff my pears, and prune the vine;
The fruit is theirs, the labour only mine.
Farewell, my pastures, my paternal stock,
My fruitful fields, and my more fruitful flock!
No more, my goats, shall I behold you climb
The steepy cliffs, or crop the flowery thyme!
No more, extended in the grot below,
Shall see you browzing on the mountain's brow
The prickly shrubs; and after on the bare,
Lean down the deep abyss, and hang in air.
No more my sheep shall sip the morning dew;
No more my song shall please the rural crew:
Adieu, my tuneful pipe! and all the world, adieu!

TITYRUS
This night, at least, with me forget your care;
Chesnuts, and curds and cream, shall be your fare:
The carpet-ground shall be with leaves o'erspread,
And boughs shall weave a covering for your head.
For see yon sunny hill the shade extends,
And curling smoke from cottages ascends.

PASTORAL II.

OR, ALEXIS.

ARGUMENT.

The commentators can by no means agree on the person of Alexis, but are all of opinion that some beautiful youth is meant by him, to whom Virgil here makes love, in Corydon's language and simplicity. His way of courtship is wholly pastoral: he complains of the boy's coyness; recommends himself for his beauty and skill in piping; invites the youth into the country, where he promises him the diversions of the place, with a suitable present of nuts and apples. But when he finds nothing will prevail, he resolves to quit his troublesome amour, and betake himself again to his former business.

Young Corydon, the unhappy shepherd swain,
The fair Alexis loved, but loved in vain;
And underneath the beechen shade, alone,
Thus to the woods and mountains made his moan:—
Is this, unkind Alexis, my reward?
And must I die unpitied, and unheard?
Now the green lizard in the grove is laid,
The sheep enjoy the coolness of the shade,
And Thestylis wild thyme and garlic beats
For harvest hinds, o'erspent with toil and heats;
While in the scorching sun I trace in vain
Thy flying footsteps o'er the burning plain.
The creaking locusts with my voice conspire,
They fried with heat, and I with fierce desire.
How much more easy was it to sustain
Proud Amaryllis, and her haughty reign,
The scorns of young Menalcas, once my care,
Though he was black, and thou art heavenly fair.
Trust not too much to that enchanting face;
Beauty's a charm, but soon the charm will pass.
White lilies lie neglected on the plain,
While dusky hyacinths for use remain.
My passion is thy scorn; nor wilt thou know
What wealth I have, what gifts I can bestow;
What stores my dairies and my folds contain—
A thousand lambs, that wander on the plain;
New milk, that all the winter never fails,
And all the summer overflows the pails.
Amphion sung not sweeter to his herd,
When summoned stones the Theban turrets reared.
Nor am I so deformed; for late I stood
Upon the margin of the briny flood:
The winds were still; and, if the glass be true,
With Daphnis I may vie, though judged by you.
O leave the noisy town! O come and see
Our country cots, and live content with me!
To wound the flying deer, and from their cotes
With me to drive a-field the browzing goats;
To pipe and sing, and, in our country strain,

To copy, or perhaps contend with Pan.
Pan taught to join with wax unequal reeds;
Pan loves the shepherds, and their flocks he feeds.
Nor scorn the pipe: Amyntas, to be taught,
With all his kisses would my skill have bought.
Of seven smooth joints a mellow pipe I have,
Which with his dying breath Damoetas gave,
And said,—"This, Corydon, I leave to thee;
For only thou deserv'st it after me."
His eyes Amyntas durst not upward lift;
For much he grudged the praise, but more the gift.
Besides, two kids, that in the valley strayed,
I found by chance, and to my fold conveyed:
They drain two bagging udders every day;
And these shall be companions of thy play;
Both fleck'd with white, the true Arcadian strain,
Which Thestylis had often begged in vain:
And she shall have them, if again she sues,
Since you the giver and the gift refuse.
Come to my longing arms, my lovely care!
And take the presents which the nymphs prepare.
White lilies in full canisters they bring,
With all the glories of the purple spring.
The daughters of the flood have searched the mead
For violets pale, and cropp'd the poppy's head,
The short narcissus and fair daffodil,
Pancies to please the sight, and cassia sweet to smell;
And set soft hyacinths with iron blue,
To shade marsh marigolds of shining hue;
Some bound in order, others loosely strowed,
To dress thy bower, and trim thy new abode.
Myself will search our planted grounds at home,
For downy peaches and the glossy plum;
And thrash the chesnuts in the neighbouring grove,
Such as my Amaryllis used to love.
The laurel and the myrtle sweets agree,
And both in nosegays shall be bound for thee.
Ah, Corydon! ah, poor unhappy swain!
Alexis will thy homely gifts disdain:
Nor, should'st thou offer all thy little store,
Will rich Iolas yield, but offer more.
What have I done, to name that wealthy swain?
So powerful are his presents, mine so mean!
The boar, amidst my crystal streams, I bring;
And southern winds to blast my flowery spring.
Ah, cruel creature! whom dost thou despise?
The gods, to live in woods, have left the skies;
And godlike Paris, in the Idæan grove,

To Priam's wealth preferred OEnone's love.
In cities, which she built, let Pallas reign;
Towers are for gods, but forests for the swain.
The greedy lioness the wolf pursues,
The wolf the kid, the wanton kid the browze;
Alexis, thou art chased by Corydon:
All follow several games, and each his own.
See, from afar, the fields no longer smoke;
The sweating steers, unharnessed from the yoke,
Bring, as in triumph, back the crooked plough;
The shadows lengthen as the sun goes low;
Cool breezes now the raging heats remove:
Ah, cruel heaven, that made no cure for love!
I wish for balmy sleep, but wish in vain;
Love has no bounds in pleasure, or in pain.
What frenzy, shepherd, has thy soul possessed?
Thy vineyard lies half pruned, and half undressed.
Quench, Corydon, thy long unanswered fire!
Mind what the common wants of life require;
On willow twigs employ thy weaving care,
And find an easier love, though not so fair.

PASTORAL III.

OR, PALÆMON.

MENALCAS, DAMOETAS, PALÆMON.

ARGUMENT.

Damoetas and Menalcas, after some smart strokes of country raillery, resolve to try who has the most skill at song; and accordingly make their neighbour, Palæmon, judge of their performances; who, after a full hearing of both parties, declares himself unfit for the decision of so weighty a controversy, and leaves the victory undetermined.

MENALCAS
Ho, swain! what shepherd owns those ragged sheep?

DAMOETAS
Ægon's they are: he gave them me to keep.

MENALCAS
Unhappy sheep, of an unhappy swain!
While he Neæra courts, but courts in vain,
And fears that I the damsel shall obtain.
Thou, varlet, dost thy master's gains devour;

Thou milk'st his ewes, and often twice an hour;
Of grass and fodder thou defraud'st the dams,
And of their mothers' dugs the starving lambs.

DAMOETAS
Good words, young catamite, at least to men.
We know who did your business, how, and when;
And in what chapel too you played your prize,
And what the goats observed with leering eyes:
The nymphs were kind, and laughed; and there your safety lies.

MENALCAS
Yes, when I cropt the hedges of the leys,
Cut Micon's tender vines, and stole the stays!

DAMOETAS
Or rather, when, beneath yon ancient oak,
The bow of Daphnis, and the shafts, you broke,
When the fair boy received the gift of right;
And, but for mischief, you had died for spite.

MENALCAS
What nonsense would the fool, thy master, prate,
When thou, his knave, canst talk at such a rate!
Did I not see you, rascal, did I not,
When you lay snug to snap young Damon's goat?
His mongrel barked; I ran to his relief,
And cried,—"There, there he goes! stop, stop the thief!"
Discovered, and defeated of your prey,
You skulked behind the fence, and sneaked away.

DAMOETAS
An honest man may freely take his own:
The goat was mine, by singing fairly won.
A solemn match was made; he lost the prize.
Ask Damon, ask, if he the debt denies.
I think he dares not; if he does, he lies.

MENALCAS
Thou sing with him? thou booby!—Never pipe
Was so profaned to touch that blubbered lip.
Dunce at the best! in streets but scarce allowed
To tickle, on thy straw, the stupid crowd.

DAMOETAS
To bring it to the trial, will you dare
Our pipes, our skill, our voices, to compare?
My brinded heifer to the stake I lay;

Two thriving calves she suckles twice a day,
And twice besides her beestings never fail
To store the dairy with a brimming pail.
Now back your singing with an equal stake.

MENALCAS
That should be seen, if I had one to make.
You know too well, I feed my father's flock;
What can I wager from the common stock?
A stepdame too I have, a cursed she,
Who rules my hen-peck'd sire, and orders me.
Both number twice a day the milky dams;
And once she takes the tale of all the lambs.
But, since you will be mad, and since you may
Suspect my courage, if I should not lay,
The pawn I proffer shall be full as good:
Two bowls I have, well turned, of beechen wood;
Both by divine Alcimedon were made;
To neither of them yet the lip is laid.
The lids are ivy; grapes in clusters lurk
Beneath the carving of the curious work.
Two figures on the sides embossed appear—
Conon, and what's his name who made the sphere,
And shewed the seasons of the sliding year,
Instructed in his trade the labouring swain,
And when to reap, and when to sow the grain?

DAMOETAS
And I have two, to match your pair, at home;
The wood the same; from the same hand they come,
(The kimbo handles seem with bear's foot carved,)
And never yet to table have been served;
Where Orpheus on his lyre laments his love,
With beasts encompassed, and a dancing grove.
But these, nor all the proffers you can make,
Are worth the heifer which I set to stake.

MENALCAS
No more delays, vain boaster, but begin!
I prophesy before-hand, I shall win.
Palæmon shall be judge how ill you rhyme:
I'll teach you how to brag another time.

DAMOETAS
Rhymer, come on! and do the worst you can;
I fear not you, nor yet a better man.
With silence, neighbour, and attention, wait;
For 'tis a business of a high debate.

PALÆMON
Sing then; the shade affords a proper place,
The trees are clothed with leaves, the fields with grass,
The blossoms blow, the birds on bushes sing,
And Nature has accomplished all the spring.
The challenge to Damoetas shall belong;
Menalcas shall sustain his under-song;
Each in his turn your tuneful numbers bring,
By turns the tuneful Muses love to sing.

DAMOETAS
From the great father of the gods above
My Muse begins; for all is full of Jove:
To Jove the care of heaven and earth belongs;
My flocks he blesses, and he loves my songs.

MENALCAS
Me Phoebus loves; for he my Muse inspires,
And in her songs the warmth he gave requires.
For him, the god of shepherds and their sheep,
My blushing hyacinths and my bays I keep.

DAMOETAS
My Phyllis me with pelted apples plies;
Then tripping to the woods the wanton hies,
And wishes to be seen before she flies.

MENALCAS
But fair Amyntas comes unasked to me,
And offers love, and sits upon my knee.
Not Delia to my dogs is known so well as he.

DAMOETAS
To the dear mistress of my love-sick mind,
Her swain a pretty present has designed:
I saw two stock-doves billing, and ere long
Will take the nest, and hers shall be the young.

MENALCAS
Ten ruddy wildings in the wood I found,
And stood on tip-toes, reaching from the ground:
I sent Amyntas all my present store;
And will, to-morrow, send as many more.

DAMOETAS
The lovely maid lay panting in my arms,
And all she said and did was full of charms.

Winds! on your wings to heaven her accents bear;
Such words as heaven alone is fit to hear.

MENALCAS
Ah! what avails it me, my love's delight,
To call you mine, when absent from my sight?
I hold the nets, while you pursue the prey,
And must not share the dangers of the day.

DAMOETAS
I keep my birth-day; send my Phyllis home;
At shearing-time, Iolas, you may come.

MENALCAS
With Phyllis I am more in grace than you;
Her sorrow did my parting steps pursue:
"Adieu, my dear!" she said, "a long adieu!"

DAMOETAS
The nightly wolf is baneful to the fold,
Storms to the wheat, to buds the bitter cold;
But, from my frowning fair, more ills I find,
Than from the wolves, and storms, and winter-wind.

MENALCAS
The kids with pleasure browze the bushy plain;
The showers are grateful to the swelling grain;
To teeming ewes the sallow's tender tree;
But, more than all the world, my love to me.

DAMOETAS
Pollio my rural verse vouchsafes to read:
A heifer, Muses, for your patron breed.

MENALCAS
My Pollio writes himself:—a bull be bred,
With spurning heels, and with a butting head.

DAMOETAS
Who Pollio loves, and who his Muse admires,
Let Pollio's fortune crown his full desires.
Let myrrh instead of thorn his fences fill,
And showers of honey from his oaks distil.

MENALCAS
Who hates not living Bavius, let him be
(Dead Mævius!) damn'd to love thy works and thee!
The same ill taste of sense would serve to join

Dog-foxes in the yoke, and shear the swine.

DAMOETAS
Ye boys, who pluck the flowers, and spoil the spring,
Beware the secret snake that shoots a sting.

MENALCAS
Graze not too near the banks, my jolly sheep;
The ground is false, the running streams are deep:
See, they have caught the father of the flock,
Who dries his fleece upon the neighbouring rock.

DAMOETAS
From rivers drive the kids, and sling your hook;
Anon I'll wash them in the shallow brook.

MENALCAS
To fold, my flock!—when milk is dried with heat,
In vain the milkmaid tugs an empty teat.

DAMOETAS
How lank my bulls from plenteous pasture come!
But love, that drains the herd, destroys the groom.

MENALCAS
My flocks are free from love, yet look so thin,
Their bones are barely covered with their skin.
What magic has bewitched the woolly dams,
And what ill eyes beheld the tender lambs?

DAMOETAS
Say, where the round of heaven, which all contains,
To three short ells on earth our sight restrains:
Tell that, and rise a Phoebus for thy pains.

MENALCAS
Nay, tell me first, in what new region springs
A flower, that bears inscribed the names of kings;
And thou shalt gain a present as divine
As Phoebus' self; for Phyllis shall be thine.

PALÆMON
So nice a difference in your singing lies,
That both have won, or both deserved the prize.
Rest equal happy both; and all who prove
The bitter sweets, and pleasing pains, of love.
Now dam the ditches, and the floods restrain;
Their moisture has already drenched the plain.

PASTORAL IV.

OR, POLLIO.

ARGUMENT.

The Poet celebrates the birth-day of Saloninus, the son of Pollio, born in the consulship of his father, after the taking of Salonæ, a city in Dalmatia. Many of the verses are translated from one of the Sibyls, who prophesied of our Saviour's birth.

Sicilian Muse, begin a loftier strain!
Though lowly shrubs, and trees that shade the plain,
Delight not all; Sicilian Muse, prepare
To make the vocal woods deserve a consul's care.
The last great age, foretold by sacred rhymes,
Renews its finished course: Saturnian times
Roll round again; and mighty years, begun
From their first orb, in radiant circles run.
The base degenerate iron offspring ends;
A golden progeny from heaven descends.
O chaste Lucina! speed the mother's pains;
And haste the glorious birth! thy own Apollo reigns!
The lovely boy, with his auspicious face,
Shall Pollio's consulship and triumph grace;
Majestic months set out with him to their appointed race.
The father banished virtue shall restore,
And crimes shall threat the guilty world no more.
The son shall lead the life of gods, and be
By gods and heroes seen, and gods and heroes see.
The jarring nations he in peace shall bind,
And with paternal virtues rule mankind.
Unbidden earth shall wreathing ivy bring,
And fragrant herbs, (the promises of spring,)
As her first offerings to her infant king.
The goats with strutting dugs shall homeward speed,
And lowing herds secure from lions feed.
His cradle shall with rising flowers be crowned:
The serpent's brood shall die; the sacred ground
Shall weeds and poisonous plants refuse to bear;
Each common bush shall Syrian roses wear.
But when heroic verse his youth shall raise,
And form it to hereditary praise,
Unlaboured harvests shall the fields adorn,
And clustered grapes shall blush on every thorn;
The knotted oaks shall showers of honey weep;

And through the matted grass the liquid gold shall creep.
Yet, of old fraud some footsteps shall remain;
The merchant still shall plough the deep for gain,
Great cities shall with walls be compassed round,
And sharpened shares shall vex the fruitful ground;
Another Tiphys shall new seas explore;
Another Argo land the chiefs upon the Iberian shore;
Another Helen other wars create,
And great Achilles urge the Trojan fate.
But when to ripened manhood he shall grow,
The greedy sailor shall the seas forego;
No keel shall cut the waves for foreign ware,
For every soil shall every product bear.
The labouring hind his oxen shall disjoin;
No plough shall hurt the glebe, no pruning-hook the vine;
Nor wool shall in dissembled colours shine;
But the luxurious father of the fold,
With native purple, and unborrowed gold,
Beneath his pompous fleece shall proudly sweat;
And under Tyrian robes the lamb shall bleat.
The Fates, when they this happy web have spun,
Shall bless the sacred clue, and bid it smoothly run.
Mature in years, to ready honours move,
O of celestial seed! O foster-son of Jove!
See, labouring Nature calls thee to sustain
The nodding frame of heaven, and earth, and main!
See to their base restored, earth, seas, and air;
And joyful ages, from behind, in crowding ranks appear.
To sing thy praise, would heaven my breath prolong,
Infusing spirits worthy such a song,
Not Thracian Orpheus should transcend my lays,
Nor Linus crowned with never-fading bays;
Though each his heavenly parent should inspire;
The Muse instruct the voice, and Phoebus tune the lyre.
Should Pan contend in verse, and thou my theme,
Arcadian judges should their god condemn.
Begin, auspicious boy! to cast about
Thy infant eyes, and, with a smile, thy mother single out.
Thy mother well deserves that short delight,
The nauseous qualms of ten long months and travail to requite.
Then smile! the frowning infant's doom is read;
No god shall crown the board, nor goddess bless the bed.

PASTORAL V.

OR, DAPHNIS.

ARGUMENT.

Mopsus and Menalcas, two very expert shepherds at a song, begin one by consent to the memory of Daphnis, who is supposed by the best critics to represent Julius Cæsar. Mopsus laments his death; Menalcas proclaims his divinity; the whole eclogue consisting of an elegy and an apotheosis.

MENALCAS
Since on the downs our flocks together feed,
And since my voice can match your tuneful reed,
Why sit we not beneath the grateful shade,
Which hazles, intermixed with elms, have made?

MOPSUS
Whether you please that sylvan scene to take,
Where whistling winds uncertain shadows make;
Or will you to the cooler cave succeed,
Whose mouth the curling vines have overspread?

MENALCAS
Your merit and your years command the choice;
Amyntas only rivals you in voice.

MOPSUS
What will not that presuming shepherd dare,
Who thinks his voice with Phoebus may compare?

MENALCAS
Begin you first; if either Alcon's praise,
Or dying Phyllis, have inspired your lays;
If her you mourn, or Codrus you commend,
Begin, and Tityrus your flock shall tend.

MOPSUS
Or shall I rather the sad verse repeat,
Which on the beeches bark I lately writ?
I writ, and sung betwixt. Now bring the swain,
Whose voice you boast, and let him try the strain.

MENALCAS
Such as the shrub to the tall olive shows,
Or the pale swallow to the blushing rose;
Such is his voice, if I can judge aright,
Compared to thine, in sweetness and in height.

MOPSUS
No more, but sit and hear the promised lay;
The gloomy grotto makes a doubtful day.

The nymphs about the breathless body wait
Of Daphnis, and lament his cruel fate.
The trees and floods were witness to their tears;
At length the rumour reached his mother's ears.
The wretched parent, with a pious haste,
Came running, and his lifeless limbs embraced.
She sighed, she sobbed; and, furious with despair,
She rent her garments, and she tore her hair,
Accusing all the gods, and every star.
The swains forgot their sheep, nor near the brink
Of running waters brought their herds to drink.
The thirsty cattle, of themselves, abstained
From water, and their grassy fare disdained.
The death of Daphnis woods and hills deplore;
They cast the sound to Libya's desert shore;
The Libyan lions hear, and hearing roar.
Fierce tigers Daphnis taught the yoke to bear,
And first with curling ivy dressed the spear.
Daphnis did rites to Bacchus first ordain,
And holy revels for his reeling train.
As vines the trees, as grapes the vines adorn,
As bulls the herds, and fields the yellow corn;
So bright a splendour, so divine a grace,
The glorious Daphnis cast on his illustrious race.
When envious Fate the godlike Daphnis took,
Our guardian gods the fields and plains forsook;
Pales no longer swelled the teeming grain,
Nor Phoebus fed his oxen on the plain;
No fruitful crop the sickly fields return,
But oats and darnel choke the rising corn;
And where the vales with violets once were crowned,
Now knotty burrs and thorns disgrace the ground.
Come, shepherds, come, and strow with leaves the plain;
Such funeral rites your Daphnis did ordain.
With cypress-boughs the crystal fountains hide,
And softly let the running waters glide.
A lasting monument to Daphnis raise,
With this inscription to record his praise:—
"Daphnis, the fields' delight, the shepherds' love,
Renowned on earth, and deified above;
Whose flock excelled the fairest on the plains,
But less than he himself surpassed the swains."

MENALCAS

O heavenly poet! such thy verse appears,
So sweet, so charming to my ravished ears,
As to the weary swain, with cares opprest,
Beneath the sylvan shade, refreshing rest;

As to the feverish traveller, when first
He finds a crystal stream to quench his thirst.
In singing, as in piping, you excel;
And scarce your master could perform so well.
O fortunate young man! at least your lays
Are next to his, and claim the second praise.
Such as they are, my rural songs I join,
To raise our Daphnis to the powers divine;
For Daphnis was so good, to love whate'er was mine.

MOPSUS
How is my soul with such a promise raised!
For both the boy was worthy to be praised,
And Stimicon has often made me long
To hear, like him, so soft, so sweet a song.

MENALCAS
Daphnis, the guest of heaven, with wondering eyes,
Views, in the milky way, the starry skies,
And far beneath him, from the shining sphere,
Beholds the moving clouds, and rolling year.
For this with cheerful cries the woods resound,
The purple spring arrays the various ground,
The nymphs and shepherds dance, and Pan himself is crowned.
The wolf no longer prowls for nightly spoils,
Nor bird's the springes fear, nor stags the toils;
For Daphnis reigns above, and deals from thence
His mother's milder beams, and peaceful influence.
The mountain-tops unshorn, the rocks, rejoice;
The lowly shrubs partake of human voice.
Assenting Nature, with a gracious nod,
Proclaims him, and salutes the new-admitted god.
Be still propitious, ever good to thine!
Behold! four hallowed altars we design;
And two to thee, and two to Phoebus rise;
On both is offered annual sacrifice.
The holy priests, at each returning year,
Two bowls of milk, and two of oil, shall bear;
And I myself the guests with friendly bowls will cheer.
Two goblets will I crown with sparkling wine,
The generous vintage of the Chian vine:
These will I pour to thee, and make the nectar thine.
In winter shall the genial feast be made
Before the fire; by summer, in the shade.
Damoetas shall perform the rites divine,
And Lyctian Ægon in the song shall join.
Alphesiboeus, tripping, shall advance,
And mimic Satyrs in his antic dance.

When to the nymphs our annual rites we pay,
And when our fields with victims we survey;
While savage boars delight in shady woods,
And finny fish inhabit in the floods;
While bees on thyme, and locusts feed on dew—
Thy grateful swains these honours shall renew.
Such honours as we pay to powers divine,
To Bacchus and to Ceres, shall be thine.
Such annual honours shall be given; and thou
Shalt hear, and shalt condemn thy suppliants to their vow.

MOPSUS
What present, worth thy verse, can Mopsus find?
Not the soft whispers of the southern wind,
That play through trembling trees, delight me more;
Nor murmuring billows on the sounding shore,
Nor winding streams, that through the valley glide,
And the scarce-covered pebbles gently chide.

MENALCAS
Receive you first this tuneful pipe, the same
That played my Corydon's unhappy flame;
The same that sung Neæra's conquering eyes,
And, had the judge been just, had won the prize.

MOPSUS
Accept from me this sheep-hook in exchange;
The handle brass, the knobs in equal range.
Antigenes, with kisses, often tried
To beg this present, in his beauty's pride,
When youth and love are hard to be denied.
But what I could refuse to his request,
Is yours unasked, for you deserve it best.

PASTORAL VI.

OR, SILENUS.

ARGUMENT.

Two young shepherds, Chromis and Mnasylus, having been often promised a song by Silenus, chance to catch him asleep in this Pastoral; where they bind him hand and foot, and then claim his promise. Silenus, finding they would be put off no longer, begins his song, in which he describes the formation of the universe, and the original of animals, according to the Epicurean philosophy; and then runs through the most surprising transformations which have happened in Nature since her birth. This Pastoral was designed as a compliment to Syron the Epicurean, who instructed Virgil and Varus in the principles of that philosophy. Silenus acts as tutor, Chromis and Mnasylus as the two pupils.

I first transferred to Rome Sicilian strains;
Nor blushed the Doric Muse to dwell on Mantuan plains.
But when I tried her tender voice, too young,
And fighting kings and bloody battles sung,
Apollo checked my pride, and bade me feed
My fattening flocks, nor dare beyond the reed.
Admonished thus, while every pen prepares
To write thy praises, Varus, and thy wars,
My pastoral Muse her humble tribute brings,
And yet not wholly uninspired she sings;
For all who read, and, reading, not disdain
These rural poems, and their lowly strain,
The name of Varus oft inscribed shall see
In every grove, and every vocal tree,
And all the sylvan reign shall sing of thee:
Thy name, to Phoebus and the Muses known,
Shall in the front of every page be shown;
For he, who sings thy praise, secures his own.
Proceed, my Muse!—Two Satyrs, on the ground,
Stretched at his ease, their sire Silenus found.
Dozed with his fumes, and heavy with his load,
They found him snoring in his dark abode,
And seized with youthful arms the drunken god.
His rosy wreath was dropt not long before,
Borne by the tide of wine, and floating on the floor.
His empty can, with ears half worn away,
Was hung on high, to boast the triumph of the day.
Invaded thus, for want of better bands,
His garland they unstring, and bind his hands;
For, by the fraudful god deluded long,
They now resolve to have their promised song.
Ægle came in, to make their party good—
The fairest Naïs of the neighbouring flood—
And, while he stares around with stupid eyes,
His brows with berries, and his temples, dyes.
He finds the fraud, and, with a smile, demands,
On what design the boys had bound his hands.
"Loose me," he cried, "'twas impudence to find
A sleeping god; 'tis sacrilege to bind.
To you the promised poem I will pay;
The nymph shall be rewarded in her way."
He raised his voice; and soon a numerous throng
Of tripping Satyrs crowded to the song;
And sylvan Fauns, and savage beasts, advanced;
And nodding forests to the numbers danced.

                    ...racian bard,
                  ...Pindus heard
                ... with more regard.
He sung... ...eeds of Nature's frame;
How seas, and earth, and air, and active flame,
Fell through the mighty void, and, in their fall,
Were blindly gathered in this goodly ball.
The tender soil then, stiffening by degrees,
Shut from the bounded earth the bounding seas.
Then earth and ocean various forms disclose,
And a new sun to the new world arose;
And mists, condensed to clouds, obscure the sky;
And clouds, dissolved, the thirsty ground supply.
The rising trees the lofty mountains grace;
The lofty mountains feed the savage race,
Yet few, and strangers, in the unpeopled place.
From thence the birth of man the song pursued,
And how the world was lost, and how renewed;
The reign of Saturn, and the golden age;
Prometheus' theft, and Jove's avenging rage;
The cries of Argonauts for Hylas drowned,
With whose repeated name the shores resound;
Then mourns the madness of the Cretan queen,—
Happy for her if herds had never been.
What fury, wretched woman, seized thy breast?
The maids of Argos, (though, with rage possessed,
Their imitated lowings filled the grove,)
Yet shunned the guilt of thy preposterous love,
Nor sought the youthful husband of the herd,
Though labouring yokes on their own necks they feared,
And felt for budding horns on their smooth foreheads reared.
Ah, wretched queen! you range the pathless wood,
While on a flowery bank he chews the cud,
Or sleeps in shades, or through the forest roves,
And roars with anguish for his absent loves.
"Ye nymphs, with toils his forest-walk surround,
And trace his wandering footsteps on the ground.
But, ah! perhaps my passion he disdains,
And courts the milky mothers of the plains.
We search the ungrateful fugitive abroad,
While they at home sustain his happy load."
He sung the lover's fraud; the longing maid,
With golden fruit, like all the sex, betrayed;
The sisters mourning for their brother's loss;
Their bodies hid in barks, and furred with moss;
How each a rising alder now appears,
And o'er the Po distils her gummy tears:
Then sung, how Gallus, by a Muse's hand,

Was led and welcomed to the sacred strand;
The senate rising to salute their guest;
And Linus thus their gratitude expressed:—
"Receive this present, by the Muses made,
The pipe on which the Ascræan pastor played;
With which of old he charmed the savage train,
And called the mountain-ashes to the plain.
Sing thou, on this, thy Phoebus; and the wood
Where once his fane of Parian marble stood:
On this his ancient oracles rehearse,
And with new numbers grace the god of verse."
Why should I sing the double Scylla's fate?
The first by love transformed, the last by hate—
A beauteous maid above; but magic arts
With barking dogs deformed her nether parts:
What vengeance on the passing fleet she poured,
The master frighted, and the mates devoured.
Then ravished Philomel the song exprest;
The crime revealed; the sisters' cruel feast:
And how in fields the lapwing Tereus reigns,
The warbling nightingale in woods complains;
While Procne makes on chimney-tops her moan,
And hovers o'er the palace once her own.
Whatever songs besides the Delphian god
Had taught the laurels, and the Spartan flood,
Silenus sung: the vales his voice rebound,
And carry to the skies the sacred sound.
And now the setting sun had warned the swain
To call his counted cattle from the plain:
Yet still the unwearied sire pursues the tuneful strain,
Till, unperceived, the heavens with stars were hung,
And sudden night surprised the yet unfinished song.

PASTORAL V.

OR, DAPHNIS.

ARGUMENT.

Meliboeus here gives us the relation of a sharp poetical contest between Thyrsis and Corydon, at which he himself and Daphnis were present; who both declared for Corydon.

Beneath a holm, repaired two jolly swains,
(Their sheep and goats together grazed the plains,)
Both young Arcadians, both alike inspired
To sing, and answer as the song required.

Daphnis, as umpire, took the middle seat,
And fortune thither led my weary feet;
For, while I fenced my myrtles from the cold,
The father of my flock had wandered from the fold.
Of Daphnis I inquired: he, smiling, said,
"Dismiss your fear;" and pointed where he fed:
"And, if no greater cares disturb your mind,
Sit here with us, in covert of the wind.
Your lowing heifers, of their own accord,
At watering time will seek the neighbouring ford.
Here wanton Mincius winds along the meads,
And shades his happy banks with bending reeds.
And see, from yon old oak that mates the skies,
How black the clouds of swarming bees arise."
What should I do? nor was Alcippe nigh,
Nor absent Phyllis could my care supply,
To house, and feed by hand my weaning lambs,
And drain the strutting udders of their dams.
Great was the strife betwixt the singing swains;
And I preferred my pleasure to my gains.
Alternate rhyme the ready champions chose:
These Corydon rehearsed, and Thyrsis those.

CORYDON
Ye Muses, ever fair, and ever young,
Assist my numbers, and inspire my song.
With all my Codrus, O! inspire my breast;
For Codrus, after Phoebus, sings the best.
Or, if my wishes have presumed too high,
And stretched their bounds beyond mortality,
The praise of artful numbers I resign,
And hang my pipe upon the sacred pine.

THYRSIS
Arcadian swains, your youthful poet crown
With ivy-wreaths; though surly Codrus frown:
Or, if he blast my Muse with envious praise,
Then fence my brows with amulets of bays,
Lest his ill arts, or his malicious tongue,
Should poison, or bewitch my growing song.

CORYDON
These branches of a stag, this tusky boar
(The first essay of arms untried before)
Young Micon offers, Delia, to thy shrine:
But, speed his hunting with thy power divine;
Thy statue then of Parian stone shall stand;
Thy legs in buskins with a purple band.

THYRSIS
This bowl of milk, these cakes, (our country fare,)
For thee, Priapus, yearly we prepare,
Because a little garden is thy care;
But, if the falling lambs increase my fold,
Thy marble statue shall be turned to gold.

CORYDON
Fair Galatea, with thy silver feet,
O, whiter than the swan, and more than Hybla sweet!
Tall as a poplar, taper as the bole!
Come, charm thy shepherd, and restore my soul!
Come, when my lated sheep at night return,
And crown the silent hours, and stop the rosy morn!

THYRSIS
May I become as abject in thy sight,
As sea-weed on the shore, and black as night;
Rough as a bur; deformed like him who chaws
Sardinian herbage to contract his jaws;
Such and so monstrous let thy swain appear,
If one day's absence looks not like a year.
Hence from the field, for shame! the flock deserves
No better feeding while the shepherd starves.

CORYDON
Ye mossy springs, inviting easy sleep,
Ye trees, whose leafy shades those mossy fountains keep,
Defend my flock! The summer heats are near,
And blossoms on the swelling vines appear.

THYRSIS
With heapy fires our cheerful hearth is crowned;
And firs for torches in the woods abound:
We fear not more the winds, and wintry cold,
Than streams the banks, or wolves the bleating fold.

CORYDON
Our woods, with juniper and chesnuts crowned,
With falling fruits and berries paint the ground;
And lavish Nature laughs, and strows her stores around:
But, if Alexis from our mountains fly,
Even running rivers leave their channels dry.

THYRSIS
Parched are the plains, and frying is the field,
Nor withering vines their juicy vintage yield:

But, if returning Phyllis bless the plain,
The grass revives, the woods are green again,
And Jove descends in showers of kindly rain.

CORYDON
The poplar is by great Alcides worn;
The brows of Phoebus his own bays adorn;
The branching vine the jolly Bacchus loves;
The Cyprian queen delights in myrtle groves;
With hazle Phyllis crowns her flowing hair;
And, while she loves that common wreath to wear,
Nor bays, nor myrtle boughs, with hazle shall compare.

THYRSIS
The towering ash is fairest in the woods;
In gardens pines, and poplars by the floods:
But, if my Lycidas will ease my pains,
And often visit our forsaken plains,
To him the towering ash shall yield in woods,
In gardens pines, and poplars by the floods.

MELIBOEUS
These rhymes I did to memory commend,
When vanquished Thyrsis did in vain contend;
Since when, 'tis Corydon among the swains:
Young Corydon without a rival reigns.

PASTORAL VIII.

OR, PHARMACEUTRIA.

ARGUMENT.

This Pastoral contains the Songs of Damon and Alphesiboeus. The first of them bewails the loss of his mistress, and repines at the success of his rival Mopsus. The other repeats the charms of some enchantress, who endeavoured, by her spells and magic, to make Daphnis in love with her.

The mournful muse of two despairing swains,
The love rejected, and the lovers' pains;
To which the savage lynxes listening stood,
The rivers stood on heaps, and stopped the running flood;
The hungry herd the needful food refuse—
Of two despairing swains, I sing the mournful muse.

Great Pollio! thou, for whom thy Rome prepares
The ready triumph of thy finished wars,

Whether Timavus or the Illyrian coast,
Whatever land or sea, thy presence boast;
Is there an hour in fate reserved for me,
To sing thy deeds in numbers worthy thee?
In numbers like to thine, could I rehearse
Thy lofty tragic scenes, thy laboured verse,
The world another Sophocles in thee,
Another Homer should behold in me.
Amidst thy laurels let this ivy twine:
Thine was my earliest muse; my latest shall be thine.

Scarce from the world the shades of night withdrew,
Scarce were the flocks refreshed with morning dew,
When Damon, stretched beneath an olive shade,
And, wildly staring upwards, thus inveighed
Against the conscious gods, and cursed the cruel maid:

"Star of the morning, why dost thou delay?
Come, Lucifer, drive on the lagging day,
While I my Nisa's perjured faith deplore,—
Witness, ye powers, by whom she falsely swore!
The gods, alas! are witnesses in vain;
Yet shall my dying breath to heaven complain.
Begin with me, my flute, the sweet Mænalian strain.

"The pines of Mænalus, the vocal grove,
Are ever full of verse, and full of love:
They hear the hinds, they hear their god complain,
Who suffered not the reeds to rise in vain
Begin with me, my flute, the sweet Mænalian strain.

"Mopsus triumphs; he weds the willing fair.
When such is Nisa's choice, what lover can despair?
Now griffons join with mares; another age
Shall see the hound and hind their thirst assuage,
Promiscuous at the spring. Prepare the lights,
O Mopsus! and perform the bridal rites.
Scatter thy nuts among the scrambling boys:
Thine is the night, and thine the nuptial joys.
For thee the sun declines: O happy swain!
Begin with me, my flute, the sweet Mænalian strain.

"O Nisa! justly to thy choice condemned!
Whom hast thou taken, whom hast thou contemned?
For him, thou hast refused my browzing herd,
Scorned my thick eye brows, and my shaggy beard.
Unhappy Damon sighs and sings in vain,
While Nisa thinks no god regards a lover's pain.

Begin with me, my flute, the sweet Mænalian strain.

"I viewed thee first, (how fatal was the view!)
And led thee where the ruddy wildings grew,
High on the planted hedge, and wet with morning dew.
Then scarce the bending branches I could win;
The callow down began to clothe my chin.
I saw; I perished; yet indulged my pain.
Begin with me, my flute, the sweet Mænalian strain.

"I know thee, Love! in deserts thou wert bred,
And at the dugs of savage tigers fed;
Alien of birth, usurper of the plains!
Begin with me, my flute, the sweet Mænalian strains.

"Relentless Love the cruel mother led
The blood of her unhappy babes to shed:
Love lent the sword; the mother struck the blow;
Inhuman she; but more inhuman thou:
Alien of birth, usurper of the plains!
Begin with me, my flute, the sweet Mænalian strains.

"Old doting Nature, change thy course anew,
And let the trembling lamb the wolf pursue;
Let oaks now glitter with Hesperian fruit,
And purple daffodils from alder shoot;
Fat amber let the tamarisk distil,
And hooting owls contend with swans in skill;
Hoarse Tityrus strive with Orpheus in the woods,
And challenge famed Arion on the floods.
Or, oh! let Nature cease, and Chaos reign!
Begin with me, my flute, the sweet Mænalian strain.

"Let earth be sea; and let the whelming tide
The lifeless limbs of luckless Damon hide:
Farewell, ye secret woods, and shady groves,
Haunts of my youth, and conscious of my loves!
From yon high cliff I plunge into the main;
Take the last present of thy dying swain;
And cease, my silent flute, the sweet Mænalian strain."

Now take your turns, ye Muses, to rehearse
His friend's complaints, and mighty magic verse:

"Bring running water; bind those altars round
With fillets, and with vervain strow the ground:
Make fat with frankincense the sacred fires,
To re-inflame my Daphnis with desires.

'Tis done: we want but verse.—Restore, my charms,
My lingering Daphnis to my longing arms.

"Pale Phoebe, drawn by verse, from heaven descends;
And Circe changed with charms Ulysses' friends.
Verse breaks the ground, and penetrates the brake,
And in the winding cavern splits the snake:
Verse fires the frozen veins.—Restore, my charms,
My lingering Daphnis to my longing arms.

"Around his waxen image first I wind
Three woollen fillets, of three colours joined;
Thrice bind about his thrice-devoted head,
Which round the sacred altar thrice is led.
Unequal numbers please the gods.—My charms,
Restore my Daphnis to my longing arms.

"Knit with three knots the fillets; knit them strait;
Then say, 'These knots to love I consecrate.'
Haste, Amaryllis, haste!—Restore, my charms,
My lovely Daphnis to my longing arms.
"As fire this figure hardens, made of clay,
And this of wax with fire consumes away;
Such let the soul of cruel Daphnis be—
Hard to the rest of women, soft to me.
Crumble the sacred mole of salt and corn:
Next in the fire the bays with brimstone burn;
And, while it crackles in the sulphur, say,
'This I for Daphnis burn; thus Daphnis burn away!
This laurel is his fate.'—Restore, my charms,
My lovely Daphnis to my longing arms.

"As when the raging heifer, through the grove,
Stung with desire, pursues her wandering love;
Faint at the last, she seeks the weedy pools,
To quench her thirst, and on the rushes rolls,
Careless of night, unmindful to return;
Such fruitless fires perfidious Daphnis burn,
While I so scorn his love!—Restore, my charms,
My lingering Daphnis to my longing arms.

"These garments once were his, and left to me,
The pledges of his promised loyalty,
Which underneath my threshold I bestow:
These pawns, O sacred earth! to me my Daphnis owe.
As these were his, so mine is he.—My charms,
Restore their lingering lord to my deluded arms.

"These poisonous plants, for magic use designed,
(The noblest and the best of all the baneful kind,)
Old Moeris brought me from the Politic strand,
And culled the mischief of a bounteous land.
Smeared with these powerful juices, on the plain,
He howls a wolf among the hungry train;
And oft the mighty necromancer boasts,
With these, to call from tombs the stalking ghosts,
And from the roots to tear the standing corn,
Which, whirled aloft, to distant fields is borne:
Such is the strength of spells.—Restore, my charms,
My lingering Daphnis to my longing arms.
"Bear out these ashes; cast them in the brook;
Cast backwards o'er your head; nor turn your look:
Since neither gods nor godlike verse can move,
Break out, ye smothered fires, and kindle smothered love.
Exert your utmost power, my lingering charms;
And force my Daphnis to my longing arms.

"See while my last endeavours I delay,
The walking ashes rise, and round our altars play!
Run to the threshold, Amaryllis,—hark!
Our Hylax opens, and begins to bark.
Good heaven! may lovers what they wish believe?
Or dream their wishes, and those dreams deceive?
No more! my Daphnis comes! no more, my charms!
He comes, he runs, he leaps, to my desiring arms."

PASTORAL IX.

OR, LYCIDAS AND MOERIS.

ARGUMENT.

When Virgil, by the favour of Augustus, had recovered his patrimony near Mantua, and went in hope to take possession, he was in danger to be slain by Arius the centurion, to whom those lands were assigned by the Emperor, in reward of his service against Brutus and Cassius. This Pastoral therefore is filled with complaints of his hard usage; and the persons introduced are the bailiff of Virgil, Moeris, and his friend Lycidas.

LYCIDAS
Ho, Moeris! whither on thy way so fast?
This leads to town.

MOERIS
O Lycidas! at last

The time is come, I never thought to see,
(Strange revolution for my farm and me!)
When the grim captain in a surly tone
Cries out, "Pack up, ye rascals, and be gone."
Kicked out, we set the best face on't we could;
And these two kids, t'appease his angry mood,
I bear,—of which the Furies give him good!

LYCIDAS
Your country friends were told another tale,—
That, from the sloping mountain to the vale,
And doddered oak, and all the banks along,
Menalcas saved his fortune with a song.

MOERIS
Such was the news, indeed; but songs and rhymes
Prevail as much in these hard iron times,
As would a plump of trembling fowl, that rise
Against an eagle sousing from the skies.
And, had not Phoebus warned me, by the croak
Of an old raven from a hollow oak,
To shun debate, Menalcas had been slain,
And Moeris not survived him, to complain.

LYCIDAS
Now heaven defend! could barbarous rage induce
The brutal son of Mars t'insult the sacred Muse?
Who then should sing the nymphs? or who rehearse
The waters gliding in a smoother verse?
Or Amaryllis praise that heavenly lay,
That shortened, as we went, our tedious way,—
"O Tityrus, tend my herd, and see them fed;
To morning pastures, evening waters, led;
And 'ware the Libyan ridgil's butting head."

MOERIS
Or what unfinished he to Varus read:—
"Thy name, O Varus, (if the kinder powers
Preserve our plains, and shield the Mantuan towers,
Obnoxious by Cremona's neighbouring crime,)
The wings of swans, and stronger-pinioned rhyme,
Shall raise aloft, and soaring bear above—
The immortal gift of gratitude to Jove."

LYCIDAS
Sing on, sing on; for I can ne'er be cloyed.
So may thy swarms the baleful yew avoid;
So may thy cows their burdened bags distend,

And trees to goats their willing branches bend.
Mean as I am, yet have the Muses made
Me free, a member of the tuneful trade:
At least the shepherds seem to like my lays;
But I discern their flattery from their praise:
I nor to Cinna's ears, nor Varus,' dare aspire,
But gabble, like a goose, amidst the swan-like choir.

MOERIS
'Tis what I have been conning in my mind;
Nor are they verses of a vulgar kind.
"Come, Galatea! come! the seas forsake!
What pleasures can the tides with their hoarse murmurs make?
See, on the shore inhabits purple spring,
Where nightingales their love-sick ditty sing:
See, meads with purling streams, with flowers the ground,
The grottoes cool, with shady poplars crowned,
And creeping vines on arbours weaved around.
Come then, and leave the waves' tumultuous roar;
Let the wild surges vainly beat the shore."

LYCIDAS
Or that sweet song I heard with such delight;
The same you sung alone one starry night.
The tune I still retain, but not the words.

MOERIS
"Why, Daphnis, dost thou search in old records,
To know the seasons when the stars arise?
See, Cæsar's lamp is lighted in the skies,—
The star, whose rays the blushing grapes adorn,
And swell the kindly ripening ears of corn.
Under this influence, graft the tender shoot;
Thy children's children shall enjoy the fruit."
The rest I have forgot; for cares and time
Change all things, and untune my soul to rhyme.
I could have once sung down a summer's sun;
But now the chime of poetry is done:
My voice grows hoarse; I feel the notes decay,
As if the wolves had seen me first to-day.
But these, and more than I to mind can bring,
Menalcas has not yet forgot to sing.

LYCIDAS
Thy faint excuses but inflame me more:
And now the waves roll silent to the shore;
Husht winds the topmost branches scarcely bend,
As if thy tuneful song they did attend:

Already we have half our way o'ercome;
Far off I can discern Bianor's tomb.
Here, where the labourer's hands have formed a bower
Of wreathing trees, in singing waste an hour.
Rest here thy weary limbs; thy kids lay down:
We've day before us yet to reach the town;
Or if, ere night, the gathering clouds we fear,
A song will help the beating storm to bear.
And, that thou may'st not be too late abroad,
Sing, and I'll ease thy shoulders of thy load.

MOERIS
Cease to request me;, let us mind our way:
Another song requires another day.
When good Menalcas comes, if he rejoice,
And find a friend at court, I'll find a voice.

PASTORAL X.

OR, GALLUS.

ARGUMENT.

Gallus, a great patron of Virgil, and an excellent poet, was very deeply in love with one Cytheris, whom he calls Lycoris, and who had forsaken him for the company of a soldier. The poet therefore supposes his friend Gallus retired, in his height of melancholy, into the solitudes of Arcadia, (the celebrated scene of pastorals,) where he represents him in a very languishing condition, with all the rural deities about him, pitying his hard usage, and condoling his misfortune.

Thy sacred succour, Arethusa, bring,
To crown my labour, ('tis the last I sing,)
Which proud Lycoris may with pity view:—
The Muse is mournful, though the numbers few.
Refuse me not a verse, to grief and Gallus due,
So may thy silver streams beneath the tide,
Unmixed with briny seas, securely glide.
Sing then my Gallus, and his hopeless vows;
Sing, while my cattle crop the tender browze.
The vocal grove shall answer to the sound,
And echo, from the vales, the tuneful voice rebound.
What lawns or woods with-held you from his aid,
Ye nymphs, when Gallus was to love betrayed,
To love, unpitied by the cruel maid?
Not steepy Pindus could retard your course,
Nor cleft Parnassus, nor the Aonian source:
Nothing, that owns the Muses, could suspend

Your aid to Gallus:—Gallus is their friend.
For him the lofty laurel stands in tears,
And hung with humid pearls the lowly shrub appears.
Mænalian pines the godlike swain bemoan,
When, spread beneath a rock, he sighed alone;
And cold Lycæus wept from every dropping stone.
The sheep surround their shepherd, as he lies:
Blush not, sweet poet, nor the name despise.
Along the streams, his flock Adonis fed;
And yet the queen of beauty blest his bed.
The swains and tardy neat-herds came, and last
Menalcas, wet with beating winter mast.
Wondering, they asked from whence arose thy flame.
Yet more amazed, thy own Apollo came.
Flushed were his cheeks, and glowing were his eyes:
"Is she thy care? is she thy care?" he cries.
"Thy false Lycoris flies thy love and thee,
And, for thy rival, tempts the raging sea,
The forms of horrid war, and heaven's inclemency."
Silvanus came: his brows a country crown
Of fennel, and of nodding lilies, drown.
Great Pan arrived; and we beheld him too,
His cheeks and temples of vermilion hue.
"Why, Gallus, this immoderate grief?" he cried,
"Think'st thou that love with tears is satisfied?
The meads are sooner drunk with morning dews,
The bees with flowery shrubs, the goats with browze."
Unmoved, and with dejected eyes, he mourned:
He paused, and then these broken words returned:—
"'Tis past; and pity gives me no relief:
But you, Arcadian swains, shall sing my grief,
And on your hills my last complaints renew:
So sad a song is only worthy you.
How light would lie the turf upon my breast,
If you my sufferings in your songs exprest!
Ah! that your birth and business had been mine—
To pen the sheep, and press the swelling vine!
Had Phyllis or Amyntas caused my pain,
Or any nymph or shepherd on the plain,
(Though Phyllis brown, though black Amyntas were,
Are violets not sweet, because not fair?)
Beneath the sallows and the shady vine,
My loves had mixed their pliant limbs with mine:
Phyllis with myrtle wreaths had crowned my hair,
And soft Amyntas sung away my care.
Come, see what pleasures in our plains abound;
The woods, the fountains, and the flowery ground.
As you are beauteous, were you half so true,

Here could I live, and love, and die with only you.
Now I to fighting fields am sent afar,
And strive in winter camps with toils of war;
While you, (alas, that I should find it so!)
To shun my sight, your native soil forego,
And climb the frozen Alps, and tread the eternal snow.
Ye frosts and snows, her tender body spare!
Those are not limbs for icicles to tear.
For me, the wilds and deserts are my choice;
The Muses, once my care; my once harmonious voice.
There will I sing, forsaken, and alone:
The rocks and hollow caves shall echo to my moan.
The rind of every plant her name shall know;
And, as the rind extends, the love shall grow.
Then on Arcadian mountains will I chase
(Mixed with the woodland nymphs) the savage race;
Nor cold shall hinder me, with horns and hounds
To thrid the thickets, or to leap the mounds.
And now methinks o'er steepy rocks I go,
And rush through sounding woods, and bend the Parthian bow;
As if with sports my sufferings I could ease,
Or by my pains the god of love appease.
My frenzy changes: I delight no more
On mountain tops to chase the tusky boar:
No game but hopeless love my thoughts pursue:
Once more, ye nymphs, and songs, and sounding woods, adieu!
Love alters not for us his hard decrees,
Not though beneath the Thracian clime we freeze,
Or Italy's indulgent heaven forego,
And in mid-winter tread Sithonian snow;
Or, when the barks of elms are scorched, we keep
On Meroë's burning plains the Libyan sheep.
In hell, and earth, and seas, and heaven above,
Love conquers all; and we must yield to Love."

My Muses, here your sacred raptures end:
The verse was what I owed my suffering friend.
This while I sung, my sorrows I deceived,
And bending osiers into baskets weaved.
The song, because inspired by you, shall shine;
And Gallus will approve, because 'tis mine—
Gallus, for whom my holy flames renew,
Each hour, and every moment rise in view;
As alders, in the spring, their boles extend,
And heave so fiercely, that the bark they rend.

Now let us rise; for hoarseness oft invades
The singer's voice, who sings beneath the shades.

From juniper unwholesome dews distil,
That blast the sooty corn, the withering herbage kill.
Away, my goats, away! for you have browzed your fill.

John Dryden – A Short Biography

John Dryden was born on August 9th, 1631 in the village rectory of Aldwincle near Thrapston in Northamptonshire, where his maternal grandfather was Rector of All Saints Church.

Dryden was the eldest of fourteen children born to Erasmus Dryden and wife Mary Pickering, paternal grandson of Sir Erasmus Dryden, 1st Baronet (1553–1632) and wife Frances Wilkes, Puritan landowning gentry who supported the Puritan cause and Parliament.

As a boy Dryden lived in the nearby village of Titchmarsh, Northamptonshire where it is probable that he received his first education.

In 1644 he was sent to Westminster School as a King's Scholar where his headmaster was Dr. Richard Busby, a charismatic teacher but severe disciplinarian. Having recently been re-founded by Elizabeth I, Westminster now embraced a very different religious and political spirit encouraging royalism and high Anglicanism but as a humanist public school, it maintained a curriculum which trained pupils in the art of rhetoric and the presentation of arguments for both sides of a given issue. This skill would remain with Dryden and influence his later writing and thinking, as much of it displays these dialectical patterns.

His first published poem, whilst still at Westminster, was an elegy with a strong royalist flavour on the death of his schoolmate Henry, Lord Hastings from smallpox, and alludes to the execution of King Charles I, which took place on January 30th, 1649.

In 1650 Dryden was ready for University and travelled to Trinity College, Cambridge. Dryden's undergraduate years would almost certainly have followed the standard curriculum of classics, rhetoric, and mathematics.

Dryden obtained his BA in 1654, graduating top of the list for Trinity that year.

However family tragedy struck in June of the same year when Dryden's father died, leaving him some land which generated a small income, but not enough to live on.

Returning to London during The Protectorate, Dryden now obtained work with Cromwell's Secretary of State, John Thurloe. This may have been the result of influence exercised on his behalf by his cousin the Lord Chamberlain, Sir Gilbert Pickering.

At Cromwell's funeral on 23 November 1658 Dryden was in the company of the Puritan poets John Milton and Andrew Marvell. The setting was to be a sea change in English history. From Republic to Monarchy and from one set of lauded poets to what would soon become the Age of Dryden.

The start began later that year when Dryden published the first of his great poems, Heroic Stanzas (1658), a eulogy on Cromwell's death which is necessarily cautious and prudent in its emotional display.

With the Restoration of the Monarchy in 1660 Dryden celebrated in verse with Astraea Redux, an authentic royalist panegyric. In this work the interregnum is illustrated as a time of anarchy, and Charles is seen as the restorer of peace and order.

With the king now established Dryden moved quickly to place himself as the leading poet and critic of his day and transferred his allegiances to the new government.

Along with Astraea Redux, Dryden welcomed the new regime with two more panegyrics: To His Sacred Majesty: A Panegyric on his Coronation (1662) and To My Lord Chancellor (1662).

These panegyrics are occasional and written to celebrate events. Thus they are written for the nation rather than the self, but these and others put him in good standing for his eventual appointment as Poet Laureate, where a number of event poems would be required each year and speaking for the Nation and to the Nation would be the first order of duty.

These poems suggest that Dryden was looking to court a possible patron which would have given him an income and time to explore his creative ideas but no, his path instead would be to make a living in writing for publishers, not for the aristocracy, and thus ultimately for the reading public.

In November 1662 Dryden was proposed for membership in the Royal Society, and he was elected an early fellow. However, his inactivity and non payment of dues led to his expulsion in 1666.

On December 1st, 1663 Dryden married the Royalist sister of Sir Robert Howard—Lady Elizabeth Howard (died 1714). The marriage was at St. Swithin's, London, and the consent of the parents is noted on the license, though Lady Elizabeth was then about twenty-five. She was the object of some scandals, well or ill founded; it was said that Dryden had been bullied into the marriage by her brothers. A small estate in Wiltshire was settled upon them by her father. The lady's intellect and temper were apparently not good; her husband was treated as an inferior by those of her social status.

Dryden's works occasionally contain outbursts against the married state but also celebrations of the same. Little else is known of the intimate side of his marriage.

Both Dryden and his wife were warmly attached to their children. They had three sons: Charles (1666–1704), John (1668–1701), and Erasmus Henry (1669–1710). Lady Elizabeth Dryden survived her husband, but went insane soon after his death and died in 1714.

With the re-opening of the theatres after the Puritan ban, Dryden began to also write plays. His first play, The Wild Gallant, appeared in 1663 but was not successful. From 1668 on he was contracted to produce three plays a year for the King's Company, in which he became a shareholder. During the 1660s and '70s, theatrical writing was his main source of income. He led the way in Restoration comedy, his best-known works being Marriage à la Mode (1672), as well as heroic tragedy and regular tragedy, in which his greatest success was All for Love (1678). Dryden was never fully satisfied with his theatrical writings and frequently suggested that his talents were wasted on unworthy audiences.

Certainly therefore fame as a poet looked more rewarding. In 1667, around the same time his dramatic career began, he published Annus Mirabilis, a lengthy historical poem which described the English defeat of the Dutch naval fleet and the Great Fire of London in 1666. It was a modern epic in pentameter quatrains that established him as the pre-eminent poet of his generation, and was crucial in his attaining the posts of Poet Laureate (1668) and then historiographer royal (1670).

When the Great Plague of London closed the theatres in 1665 Dryden retreated to Wiltshire where he wrote Of Dramatick Poesie (1668), arguably the best of his unsystematic prefaces and essays. Dryden constantly defended his own literary practice, and Of Dramatick Poesie, the longest of his critical works, takes the form of a dialogue in which four characters—each based on a prominent contemporary, with Dryden himself as 'Neander'—debate the merits of classical, French and English drama.

He felt strongly about the relation of the poet to tradition and the creative process, and his heroic play Aureng-zebe (1675) has a prologue which denounces the use of rhyme in serious drama. His play All for Love (1678) was written in blank verse, and was to immediately follow Aureng-Zebe.

On December 18th, 1679 he was attacked in Rose Alley near his home in Covent Garden by thugs hired by fellow poet, John Wilmot, 2nd Earl of Rochester, with whom he had a long-standing conflict. Wilmot was constantly in and out of favour with the King and his own poetry was often bawdy, lewd, even obscene and made fun of the King who would often exile him from Court.

Dryden's greatest achievements were in satiric verse: the mock-heroic Mac Flecknoe, a more personal product of his Laureate years, was a lampoon circulated in manuscript and an attack on the playwright Thomas Shadwell. Dryden's main goal in the work is to "satirize Shadwell, ostensibly for his offenses against literature but more immediately we may suppose for his habitual badgering of him on the stage and in print." It is not a belittling form of satire, but rather one which makes his object great in ways which are unexpected, transferring the ridiculous into poetry. This line of satire continued with Absalom and Achitophel (1681) and The Medal (1682). Other major works from this period are the religious poems Religio Laici (1682), written from the position of a member of the Church of England; his 1683 edition of Plutarch's Lives, translated From the Greek by Several Hands in which he introduced the word biography to English readers; and The Hind and the Panther, (1687) which celebrates his conversion to Roman Catholicism.

He wrote Britannia Rediviva celebrating the birth of a son and heir to the Catholic King and Queen on June 10th, 1688. When later in the same year James II was deposed in the Glorious Revolution, Dryden's refusal to take the oaths of allegiance to the new monarchs, William and Mary, which left him out of favour at court and he had to leave his post as Poet Laureate. Thomas Shadwell, his despised rival, succeeded him. Dryden, England's greatest literary figure, was now forced to give up his public offices and live by the proceeds of his pen alone.

Dryden was an excellent translator with his own style which brought the ire of many critics. Many felt he would embellish or expand anything he felt short or curt. Dryden did not feel such expansion was a fault, arguing that as Latin is a naturally concise language it cannot be duly represented by a comparable number of words in the much larger English vocabulary. He continued with his task of translating works by Horace, Juvenal, Ovid, Lucretius, and Theocritus, a task which he found far more satisfying than writing for the stage.

In 1694 he began work on what would be his most ambitious and defining work as translator, The Works of Virgil (1697), which was published by subscription. The publication of the translation of Virgil was a national event and brought Dryden the sum of £1,400.

His final translations appeared in the volume Fables Ancient and Modern (1700), a series of episodes from Homer, Ovid, and Boccaccio, as well as modernised adaptations from Geoffrey Chaucer interspersed with Dryden's own poems. As a translator, he made great literary works in the older languages available to readers of English.

John Dryden died on May 12th, 1700, and was initially buried in St. Anne's cemetery in Soho, before being exhumed and reburied in Westminster Abbey ten days later. He was the subject of poetic eulogies, such as Luctus Brittannici: or the Tears of the British Muses; for the Death of John Dryden, Esq. (London, 1700), and The Nine Muses.

He is seen as dominating the literary life of Restoration England to such a point that the period came to be known in literary circles as the Age of Dryden. Walter Scott called him "Glorious John."

Dryden was the dominant literary figure and influence of his age. He established the heroic couplet as a standard form of English poetry by writing successful satires, religious pieces, fables, epigrams, compliments, prologues, and plays with it; he also introduced the alexandrine and triplet into the form. In his poems, translations, and criticism, he established a poetic diction appropriate to the heroic couplet—Auden referred to him as "the master of the middle style"—that was a model for his contemporaries and for much of the 18th century. The considerable loss felt by the English literary community at his death was evident in the elegies written about him. Dryden's heroic couplet went on to become the dominant poetic form of the 18th century.

What Dryden achieved in his poetry was neither the emotional excitement of the early nineteenth-century romantics nor the intellectual complexities of the metaphysicals. Although he uses formal structures such as heroic couplets, he tried to recreate the natural rhythm of speech, and he knew that different subjects need different kinds of verse. In his preface to Religio Laici he says that "the expressions of a poem designed purely for instruction ought to be plain and natural, yet majestic... The florid, elevated and figurative way is for the passions; for (these) are begotten in the soul by showing the objects out of their true proportion.... A man is to be cheated into passion, but to be reasoned into truth."

Perhaps the following illustrates Dryden and his life—"The way I have taken, is not so streight as Metaphrase, nor so loose as Paraphrase: Some things too I have omitted, and sometimes added of my own. Yet the omissions I hope, are but of Circumstances, and such as wou'd have no grace in English; and the Addition, I also hope, are easily deduc'd from Virgil's Sense. They will seem (at least I have the Vanity to think so), not struck into him, but growing out of him".

John Dryden – A Concise Bibliography

Astraea Redux, 1660
The Wild Gallant (comedy), 1663
The Indian Emperour (tragedy), 1665
Annus Mirabilis (poem), 1667
The Enchanted Island (comedy), 1667, with William D'Avenant from Shakespeare's The Tempest
Secret Love, or The Maiden Queen, 1667
An Essay of Dramatick Poesie, 1668

An Evening's Love (comedy), 1668
Tyrannick Love (tragedy), 1669
The Conquest of Granada, 1670
The Assignation, or Love in a Nunnery, 1672
Marriage à la mode, 1672
Amboyna, or the Cruelties of the Dutch to the English Merchants, 1673
The Mistaken Husband (comedy), 1674
Aureng-zebe, 1675
All for Love, 1678
Oedipus (heroic drama), 1679, an adaptation with Nathaniel Lee of Sophocles' Oedipus
Absalom and Achitophel, 1681
The Spanish Fryar, 1681
Mac Flecknoe, 1682
The Medal, 1682
Religio Laici, 1682
To the Memory of Mr. Oldham, 1684
Threnodia Augustalis, 1685
The Hind and the Panther, 1687
A Song for St. Cecilia's Day, 1687
Britannia Rediviva, 1688, written to mark the birth of a Prince of Wales.
Amphitryon, 1690
Don Sebastian (play), 1690
Creator Spirit, by whose aid, 1690. Translation of Rabanus Maurus' Veni Creator Spiritus
King Arthur, 1691
Cleomenes, 1692
The Art of Satire, 1693
Love Triumphant, 1694
The Works of Virgil, 1697
Alexander's Feast, 1697
Fables, Ancient and Modern, 1700

www.ingramcontent.com/pod-product-compliance
Lightning Source LLC
Chambersburg PA
CBHW072306160225
22055CB00010B/1115